THE METHODOLOGY OF ECONOMIC
MODEL BUILDING

The Methodology of Economic Model Building

Methodology after Samuelson

Lawrence A. Boland

ROUTLEDGE
London and New York

First published 1989
by Routledge
11 New Fetter Lane, London EC4P 4EE
29 West 35th Street, New York, NY 10001

© 1989 Lawrence A. Boland

Printed in Great Britain by
Billing & Sons Ltd, Worcester

British Library Cataloguing in Publication Data

Boland, Lawrence A.
  The methodology of economic model
  building: methodology after Samuelson.
  1. Economic models. Design & applications
  I. Title
  330'.0724

  ISBN 0-415-00014-9

Library of Congress Cataloging in Publication Data

Boland, Lawrence A.
  The methodology of economic model building.

  Bibliography: p.
  Includes indexes.
  1. Economics — Methodology. 2. Samuelson, Paul
Anthony, 1915–   . I. Title.
HB131.B65   1988   330'.01'8   88-23919
ISBN 0-415-00014-9

To Joske, my unofficial senior supervisor

Contents

Contents

Acknowledgements

I wish to thank many people for taking the time to read the manuscript of this book. Those deserving particular praise are Irene Gordon, Paul Harrald, Soren Lemche and Donna Wilson for their significant advice and criticism. My friends Peter Kennedy, Abdelkrim Errouaki, Kevin Hoover, Nancy Wulwick and Shayam Kamath are to be commended for their gallant efforts towards setting me straight with regard to Chapter 8 and Robert Jones for his careful examination of Chapters 2 and 3. Since much of this book was developed over a period of twenty-five years in my many methodology seminars at Simon Fraser University, I would like to acknowledge my students and friends, Geoffrey Newman, Wayne Pack and Kathryn Goddard who provided the support and criticism that I needed to understand the methodologically important questions.

In addition, I wish to thank the editors of the three journals who were willing to publish the original versions of some of the chapters included here. A shorter version of Chapter 6 was published by the **Atlantic Economic Journal**. Chapters 4 and 5 are revised versions of articles that appeared in **Philosophy of Science**. Earlier versions of Chapters 1 and 7 (as well as Section 3, Chapter 3) were published by the **South African Journal of Economics**. Finally, I thank the current editors of these journals for their permission to use copyright material.

Preface

Does testability of a model really matter in economics? How would one know whether testability can ever matter? Why should testability matter to a model builder? These are the key questions addressed in this book. They involve the lofty concerns of methodology as well as the more mundane matters of model building itself.

In the past twenty-five years I have read or listened to hundreds of papers on economic theory or applied economics. I do not recall an author ever saying something like, 'I chose not to use a Cobb-Douglas production function because it would make my model less testable'. If testability really matters to economic model builders then there ought to be evidence which shows that the extent to which a chosen assumption affected the testability of a model was a determining factor in its use. Frankly, I doubt whether any model builder ever takes into account what a given modelling assumption does to the testability of his or her model despite all the lip-service given to high-sounding methodological pronouncements regarding the importance of testability.

Testability, of course, does not represent all methodological issues in economics nor does model building represent all activities in economics. In this book I have focused exclusively on these two topics as objects of a research programme in applied methodology. In effect, this book reports the results of that programme which has occupied my writing and research for more than twenty-five years. As a methodologist I try to be self-conscious. Whenever I discuss methodology, I find that I almost always need to talk also about how to study methodology. For example, since I am reporting specific results of a research programme in applied methodology, I feel compelled to report what I learned about research programmes in general, as well as about meta-methodology. This can be confusing both for me and the audience, so I have tried to separate applications from the general lessons.

The lessons I have learned about methodology as a research topic are discussed separately in the Prologue and the Epilogue of this book. The primary lesson was that methodologists are often misled by philosophers and can learn more by trying to understand what methodologically aware economists have to say. The Prologue and Epilogue are then merely slices of bread surrounding the meat. The 'meat', which comprises Chapters 1 to 8, presents all that I have learned about the role and application of testability in economic model building. The main finding is that if testability were as important as most model builders claim, very little in economic theory and model building would see the light of day. While none of the chapters are reprints, it should be noted that some of the 'meat' presented here is reprocessed. Specifically, earlier versions of Chapters 1 and 4 through 7 have been published. The remaining chapters are new or have not been published: Chapters 2 and 3 are adaptations of my unpublished PhD thesis and Chapter 8 is almost entirely new with only a few sentences reappearing from an earlier reply to some of my critics. Everything previously published has been rewritten so as to form a coherent whole.

As a beginning academic in the 1960s working on applied methodology, there were very few journals in the world which would publish my work. In fact, I had 55 rejections before my first article was published in 1968. I learned a lot from those rejections. While I would have preferred to publish in the AER or the JPE, at first only the SAJE was willing to put my work into print. By now things have changed and it is much easier to find someone to publish methodology although the JPE and the AER still do not find much room for it.

I have written this book for two audiences. The primary audience is intended to be anyone who is interested in the specific question of how testability matters in economic model building. The secondary audience is envisaged as that growing band of young would-be methodologists who I think *ought* to be more concerned with how grand notions about methodology actually affect the practice of economics than with whether philosophers will turn their heads to listen. For this secondary audience the book should be seen as a case study. For the primary audience I think I have provided ample evidence that methodological concerns do matter in the everyday affairs of economic model builders and moreover, that model builders ought not to take methodology for granted.

L.A.B.
Burnaby, British Columbia
9 March 1988

PROLOGUE

Methodology vs Applied Methodology

What methodology can do is to provide criteria for the
acceptance and rejections of research programs, setting
standards that will help us to discriminate between wheat
and chaff. These standards ... are hierarchical, relative,
dynamic, and by no means unambiguous in terms of the
practical advice they offer to working economists.

Mark Blaug [1980, p. 264]

Economists do not follow the laws of enquiry their
methodologies lay down. A good thing, too.

Donald N. McCloskey [1983, p. 482]

This book is a methodological examination of model building in
modern economics. The act of building a model in economic
theory always involves methodological decisions on the part of the
model builder. Such decisions are sometimes about large
questions, such as whether to build an econometric model to deal
with existing empirical data or an abstract mathematical model
which ignores empirical data. At other times decisions about more
mundane questions must be made such as whether to use ordinary
least-squares or two-stage least-squares or to use simple linear
models rather than more complex models using non-linear
functions. As these decisions always depend on the intended
purpose for the model, there are very few salient methodological
principles for model building in general. Nevertheless, over the
last thirty years a few common concerns of model builders have
evolved. A central issue has been the concern for the testability of
economic models. While some philosophers have made sweeping
pronouncements on the question of testability, hardly anybody has
examined the basis for making methodological decisions in modern

1

economics. How a practicing model builder in modern economics deals with the question of testability and similar methodological questions is critically examined in this book.

1. Model building in modern economics

Almost all recent textbooks in economics include frequent references to 'models'. In modern social sciences the methodology of 'model building' has virtually excluded the older, more literary approaches to analysis. Although model building in the more advanced textbooks involves considerable use of mathematics, the concept of a model is more elementary and also more common. For example, there are fashion models, model homes, model students, model airplanes, design models, prototype models, and so on. Let us consider what these have in common.

Models are somehow neither 'realistic' nor ordinary – usually they are, in some way, artificial. Models are the outcomes of conscious efforts on the part of model builders. All models are models of some*thing*. In academic studies that something is usually a theory or explanation of some phenomena.[1] The methodology of model building focuses on the *adequacy* of any given model. However, 'adequacy' is not an absolute or universal criterion. The adequacy of a model can be judged only in terms of the model's intended purpose or the aims of the model builder. The purposes for building models seem to fall into two general categories:

(1) *Pure* or *abstract models* which are representations of the underlying logic of the theory being modelled,

(2) *Applied models* which are explicit, simplified representations of more general theories and which are designed to apply to specific real-world problems or situations.

In addition, there are two different types of applied models: models of explanation and models for deriving policy recommen-

---

[1] It should be noted here that in economics literature there are differences in how models are distinguished from theories. The difference used in this book corresponds to the usage in engineering literature – models are more specific or particular than the theories being modelled. Mathematical logicians give the opposite meaning. In their literature, a model represents the meaningless logic underlying a theory such that the theory amounts to a specific interpretation of the logic of the model [e.g. see Papandreou 1958 and Bronfenbrenner 1966].

dations. To a significant extent there is an abstract model underlying every applied model and the interaction between them will be the focus of our attention throughout this book.

1.1. An example of an abstract model used in economics

The most common abstract model used in economics is that of 'maximizing behaviour'. Producers are alleged to be 'profit maximizers' and consumers are alleged to be 'utility maximizers'. Although they have the simple idea of maximization in common, most textbooks have a chapter on the behaviour of the consumer and another chapter on the behaviour of the producer (the firm). Both chapters go through all the logic of maximization but each uses different words. Alternatively, some textbooks discuss the logic of maximization in general and then deal with the consumer's situation and the producer's situation, each as a special case. This latter approach, which has been used many times in recent years, involves the building of an abstract model, usually the one based on the logic of maximization [e.g. Samuelson 1947/65].

Before considering an abstract model of the generic maximizer, I would like to develop one of the specific 'special cases' so we can be sure that we know what the abstract model is supposed to represent. Let us look at elementary consumer theory.

Economists have a view that every consumer considers all the quantities of any particular good, say tomatoes, that he or she could buy, given his or her tomato budget and the price of tomatoes, and then buys the one quantity which maximizes his or her 'utility' (i.e. the total measure of satisfaction the consumer will experience from eating the tomatoes purchased). To make the choice easier, let us say the consumer can have as many tomatoes as he or she wants (i.e. tomatoes are free). However, let us also say that the consumer must eat all the tomatoes chosen within a specified amount of time, say four hours. The economist says that the consumer will thus choose the one quantity of tomatoes which maximizes his or her utility, neither more nor less. Generally, the consumer will not eat all the available tomatoes.

For the most part, what an economist has to say about the behaviour of any consumer is merely a logical consequence of the assertion that the consumer is a 'utility maximizer'. This view, for example, says that whenever the consumer *is maximizing* his or her utility while facing an unlimited budget for tomatoes (or when tomatoes are free), it must be the case that the consumer has chosen that quantity of tomatoes, say 10 pounds, such that if the consumer were to eat one *more* tomato, his or her total satisfaction (measured on some scale which we call 'utility') would decrease. Economists express this by saying the marginal utility of an extra tomato will be negative. Economists also say that for each pound up to the chosen 10 pounds, the consumer's total satisfaction increases with each additional pound. That is, the consumer's marginal utility is positive for each additional pound up to the tenth pound. Since (as they say) marginal utility is positive for each additional pound below ten and negative for each additional pound over ten, usually we can also conclude that the marginal utility must be zero at 10 pounds.

There are three distinct ideas used in this elementary *theory* of the tomato consumer facing unlimited choice.

The assumption that:

(a) utility is being maximized by the choice of the quantity of tomatoes.

The conclusions that:

(b) marginal utility is zero at the chosen quantity of tomatoes,
(c) marginal utility falls as the quantity of tomatoes rises.

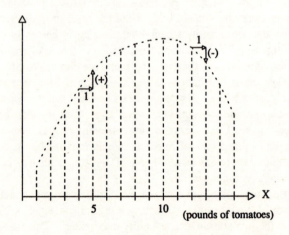

Figure 1 *Maximization Model*

It is said that (b) and (c) are logical consequences of (a). That is, if the condition of utility and chosen quantity are as indicated by (a) then *necessarily* both ideas (b) and (c) are true.

There are many different *models* of such a theory. They are different only because we choose to represent the basic ideas of the theory in different ways. Most often economists use diagrams to represent their ideas. In this elementary consumer theory case, the level of utility is represented with a diagram on which we record the levels of satisfaction or 'utility' that would be obtained by the consumer at each given amount of a good (see Figure 1). The curved dotted line connecting all the recorded points is supposedly determined by the consumer's psychologically given 'utility function'.

Whenever we say the consumer chooses 10 pounds of tomatoes because at 10 pounds his or her utility is maximized, we can represent that choice on the diagram by using the numbers along the horizontal axis to represent 'pounds of tomatoes' (i.e. X equals the 'quantity of tomatoes') and positioning the utility function such that the maximum occurs at $X = 10$, representing 10 pounds. This implies that the consumer is free to choose any quantity he or she wants. It is easy to see that ideas (b) and (c) will follow straight from this diagram. To the left of 10 pounds, as each pound is added to the quantity of tomatoes (e.g. the fifth pound), the total utility gets higher, i.e. the level of satisfaction received changes by a positive amount. This means, according to our diagram, that the marginal utility (MU) to the left of 10 pounds is positive. We can also note that for each additional pound, the amount by which the total utility goes up is less and less as we get closer to 10 pounds. From this we can conclude that 'marginal utility falls with rising quantity of tomatoes', i.e. idea (c) above. And since not only is the marginal utility to the right of 10 pounds negative, for a very small change in the neighbourhood of 10 pounds, it would be very difficult to detect any change in utility and thus we can say that marginal utility is zero at the chosen quantity of tomatoes, i.e. idea (b) above.

The above conclusions follow from the geometrical properties of our diagram and they would hold for *maximization* in general. That is, calling the horizontal scale 'pounds of tomatoes' is a specific model of the utility maximizing consumer. Thus we see that one possible *abstract* or *pure* model of utility maximizing consumers is merely the logic of the geometrical properties of the diagram without any labels on the axes. The logic of the diagram is more general than the specific case of choosing *tomatoes* in order to maximize *utility*. The logic holds for *any* case of maximizing any measure with respect to any product. Whether or not utility maximization is a true theory for the choice of tomatoes is a separate matter. Abstract models are intended to be true for all cases for which they apply but specific models may be true only for the case represented (e.g. for the choice of tomatoes but maybe not for wine).

1.2. Models of explanation and policy recommendations

In economics, we say that every explanation is of some (observable or observed) events. Each of these events is described as one of the many possible values or states for each of a specified set of variables (called *endogenous* variables since they are supposedly determined logically *within* the model explaining their values). The explanation of the particular observed events (or values) requires *both* another set of variables, each of which has many possible values or states (these are called the *exogenous* variables since their values are determined *outside* or independently of the model), *and* one or more universal principles (e.g. behavioural assumptions) relating to the two sets of variables in some specific way. The two sets of variables are distinguished only as follows: Endogenous variables are alleged to be *influenced* by exogenous variables as indicated by the universal principles, *but* exogenous variables are alleged *not* to be influenced by endogenous variables in any way. In this sense the exogenous set is called the 'givens' or sometimes the 'initial conditions'. Now an explanation of one or more events (each represented by a list where there is one value for each endogenous variable) is accomplished by showing that, by means of the universal principles, *only those* events are logically compatible with a specified list of values, i.e. a list with one value for each exogenous 'given'. The explanations are considered successful when the actual (observed) values of the 'givens' correspond to the logically necessary set of values. A different set of (observed) events would be compatible *only* with a different set of 'givens'.

In the case of explaining a change in any endogenous variable (i.e. a change to a different list of values), we are limited, by the logic of this theory of explanation, to explaining a change as being the result of some change in the values of one or more of the exogenous 'givens'.

Exogeneity is an asserted attribute of variables – it is not usually a property of the logical structure of a model. By itself, an equation of a model cannot represent exogeneity. Very often students find that it is possible to manipulate one or more equations of a simple macro-economic model and produce an equation which would *appear* to indicate that the observed values of the exogenous variables are determined by the observed values of the endogenous variables. Such an *interpretation* of an equation would contradict the intended meaning of exogeneity attributed to those variables.[2]

Recognition of the distinction between exogenous and endogenous variables is crucial in the building of models of the economy whenever those models are to be used as the basis for policy recommendations. One good reason why some variables are exogenous is that they are totally controlled by some autonomous institution or individual. Some examples of exogenous variables of this type might be tax rates, the level of advertising, the government's budget, private investment or loans, and so on. These are examples of potential policy implements. Policy questions are about what would be the benefit or cost of changing one or more of these variables. For example, what would happen to the rate of inflation if the government changed the tax rate? If the tax rate were not an exogenous variable, this would be a meaningless question. We can talk only about directly changing something over which we have control.

In summary, when building models for either explanation or for policy recommendations, some variables must be exogenous. We

---

[2] To illustrate, let us say that over the past ten years we observe that the average price of wheat each year has been inversely proportional to the amount of rainfall per year. We can put that in the form of a simple equation which would tell how to calculate the average price whenever you know what the expected rainfall is:

$$P_W = A/R$$

In this equation, P_W represents the average price of wheat, R represents the annual rainfall measured in centimetres and A is a fixed proportionality parameter which translates centimetres into dollar prices. As a matter of algebraic (or logical) manipulations alone, we could reverse or 'solve' this equation for R and get:

$$R = A/P_W$$

Now, even though we can solve or reverse the equation for P_W to make it an equation for R, we cannot interpret either to mean 'the price of wheat determines the level of rainfall'. Stated another way, rainfall is an exogenous variable. It might make sense to say the level of rainfall influences the price of wheat, but it usually would not make sense to say that the price of wheat influences the level of rainfall.

cannot build models with only endogenous variables. Saying that there *must* be some exogenous variables means that we can never expect to be able to explain everything. And going further, exogeneity by itself does not imply control. If we want to make policy recommendations with the explanatory models we build, some of the needed exogenous variables must represent variables over which someone has control. Deciding which variables are to be included in a model, and deciding which of them are to be exogenous, are the most fundamental methodological decisions that a model builder must make.

2. Methodology as a study of model-building methods

Since the early 1960s, graduate education in economics has been increasingly devoted to teaching the modelling methods that are widely accepted in the economics profession. It is all too easy for graduate students to reach the conclusion that the best graduate programmes are those that teach the most up-to-date modelling methods. And given such proclivities, when the graduate students become teachers, it is too inviting for them to try to convince their undergraduate students that there must be only one approved method. Some even turn to the study of methodology in hopes that philosophers can add support to their current choice of an approved modelling method.

When I was an undergraduate student of economics I read a book by Henry Briefs, **Three Views of Method in Economics** [1960], which I found liberating. For the first time I was encouraged to dismiss the common philosophical notion that there must be only one correct and authoritative method for economics and was free to consider many views of economic methodology. The feeling of liberation was due more to the rejection of the authoritarianism of most methodologists than to the specific views of method that Briefs discussed in his book.

While, morally speaking, one ought to allow for a plurality of reasonable views, such 'pluralism' can be debilitating. What if economists had to simultaneously allow that individual decision-makers can be assumed to be maximizers, non-maximizers and satisficers? Surely, economists wishing to apply economic theory would reach an insurmountable impasse. While some economic theorists might be able to survive by allowing for all possible behavioural assumptions, every applied economist learns quickly that to succeed he or she must adopt one position (e.g. one behavioural assumption) and give it a whirl.

Despite the efforts of many methodologists and philosophers, working economists eschew most disputes over the realism of their assumptions. The proof of the assumed pudding, they say, is always in the eating – or more specifically, in the results of the modelling based on an assumption in question. If you think you have a more realistic assumption, they will tell you to build a model using it and show that it yields superior results. By analogy, I think one can also say that if you think you have a superior methodology then show us. Apply that methodology to some important model building process and show that it yields superior models. Even if you are not convinced that you have found the world's best methodology, to practice economics you must adopt a single methodology. This book is about the application of one particular methodological approach to model building in economics. It is about the one methodological rule which has dominated economics since the early 1960s. The rule at issue is the methodological requirement that all economic models or theories, if they are going to be given serious consideration by practicing economists, must be shown to be testable where a successful test of a theory is defined as a falsification of that theory. A testable theory is a falsifiable theory.

2.1. Testability as falsifiability in economics

The methodological requirement of falsifiability is so common-place today that it is difficult for most of us to think of economists ever putting forth theories or models that are not falsifiable. Falsifiability (or equivalently, refutability) was certainly in the air even during the 'years of high theory' (i.e. the 1930s). Most historians of economic thought credit Terrence Hutchison's 1938 book, **The Significance and Basic Postulates of Economic Theory**, with the explicit introduction of the methodological requirement of falsifiability to economics. Hutchison refers often to the philosopher Karl Popper in explaining the nature and significance of falsifiability. According to Popper, and in opposition to the commonplace view of his time, falsifiability rather than verifiability was to be stressed as the primary attribute that makes theories scientific. At about the same time (1937), Paul Samuelson introduced to economics a different methodological requirement – namely the requirement that economic models and theories must be 'operationally meaningful'. As Samuelson defines the issue,

> By a meaningful theorem I mean simply a hypothesis about empirical data which could conceivably be refuted, if only under ideal conditions. A meaningful theorem may be false. [Samuelson 1947/65, p. 4]

Unlike Hutchison, Samuelson makes no reference to Popper or any other philosopher to explain why falsifiability is methodologically important.

Hutchison's pronouncements did not seem to have much effect on the economics profession and Samuelson's contribution to economic methodology did not appear in print until 1947. But even as late as the mid-1950s, verifiability still held the attention of many economic methodologists [see Machlup 1955; Hutchison 1956]. However, a specific effort to make empirical testing central to economics and economic methodology was made by a group of young economists at the London School of Economics (LSE). The venue was the 'Staff Seminar on Methodology, Measurement, and Testing in Economics' [see de Marchi 1985/88]. For some reason, the idea of empirical testing was subsumed under the flag of 'positive economics'. While one of the members of the seminar, Richard Lipsey, made empirical testability a central concern of his 1963 textbook **An Introduction to Positive Economics**, another member, Chris Archibald, was pleading for a more palatable alternative to the severe requirement of empirical refutability [Archibald 1966].

Since the first edition (1961) of his famous textbook on the history of thought, **Economic Theory in Retrospect**, Mark Blaug has continued to promote falsifiability as the operative methodological rule in economics, culminating in his 1980 book, **The Methodology of Economics**, which expanded on the earlier textbook's treatment of methodology. Blaug makes an important distinction. He notes that 'economists frequently preach falsificationism … but they rarely practice it' [1980, p. 128]. Note carefully that for Blaug, any practice of what he calls falsificationism amounts not only to devising models which are in principle refutable but also to actively attempting to refute such models. With the possible exception of a brief moment in the LSE seminar, hardly any mainstream economists have advocated such a strict employment of the Popper-Samuelson methodological requirement of falsifiability. The view that anyone who advocates the employment of a requirement of falsifiability must also be advocating the pursuit of falsifying tests is a mistake, which incorrectly attributes concern for falsifiability exclusively to popular (mis)interpretations of Popper's philosophy of science. For practicing model builders, the issue of required falsifiability has more to do with avoiding vacuous tautologies than with philosophical concerns over the true purposes of science. Avoiding tautologies is quite explicit in Hutchison's 1938 book and the above quotation from Samuelson's 1947 book clearly shows that he thought by requiring refutability he was thereby assuring that theorems can be false. To say a statement can be false is just another way of saying that it is necessarily not a tautology.

So, the fact that mainstream economists advocate the methodological requirement of falsifiability yet do not spend all their time attempting to refute mainstream economic theories or models does not constitute an integrity failure as Blaug seems to suggest. It merely means that economists are more interested in what Samuelson had to say about methodology than what philosophers such as Karl Popper might think the purpose of economic science should be.

2.2. *Against methodology as the study of Big Questions*

The widespread adoption of the methodological requirement of falsifiability, whether it be implicit or explicit, makes an interesting topic for a research programme in economic methodology. But given the depth of concern for the philosophical aspects of the Popper-Samuelson requirement of falsifiability, it is important to keep the philosophical questions in proper perspective. Modesty and humility are essential for any methodological study of practicing economists.

Despite what a few well-intentioned methodologists have been arguing recently [e.g. Caldwell 1982], there is very little that an ordinary philosopher can do to help the typical model builder in economics. While Plato, Descartes or John Stuart Mill may have had profound ideas about the nature and purpose of human thought, such profound ideas will not likely help the practicing economist who is attempting to measure the level of unemployment in the forest industry or who is attempting to determine if individual utility maximization is consistent with the market determination of prices.

Unfortunately, one of the reasons why most people study methodology is that they are interested in the Big Questions about the nature and purposes of human activity. They are interested in what Don McCloskey [1983] would call 'Methodology with a capital M'. Very little has been published about lower-case methodology – i.e. the practical methodology of the practicing economist. Of course, it is somewhat risky to write about practical methodology since there may not be an audience. The ordinary philosopher or upper-case Methodologist will not find practical (lower-case) methodology of any interest since it never seems to answer Big Questions, and practicing economists will turn away because they think all methodology is restricted to the theory of Big Questions.

The schism between practice and theory has haunted academic economists for many decades. Alfred Marshall attempted to bridge the gap in 1890 with his famous **Principles of Economics**. John Maynard Keynes attempted the same thing in 1936 with his famous **General Theory of Employment, Interest and Money**. With their 1958 book, **Linear Programming and Economic Analysis**, Robert Dorfman, Paul Samuelson and Robert Solow tried to explain existence proofs and fixed-point theorems to the average business graduate student. While these books have been successful in the wider sense, none of them seems to have built a strong enough bridge and the schism remains.

One sees this schism clearest when it comes to using economic theory as a policy guide for governmental agencies. Consider Alain Enthoven's view of economic analysis in the US Department of Defense:

> the tools of analysis that we [government economists] ... use are the simplest, most fundamental concepts of economic theory, combined with the simplest quantitative methods. The requirements for success in this line of work are a thorough understanding of and, if you like, belief in the relevance of such concepts as marginal products and costs in complex situations, combined with a good quantitative sense. The economic theory we are using is the theory most of us learned as sophomores. [Enthoven 1963, p. 422]

After conducting a survey of governmental economists, William R. Allen observed that:

> In performing their chores ... government economists are subject to various constraints ... [T]he world of the government economist

12

can be, and typically is, very different in important respects from the world of the academic economist.

No one seriously disputed the essence of [Enthoven's] characterization of governmental economics work done in the early 1960's.
And few believed that the level of rigor and technical sophistication
in economics ... had increased strikingly during the following
decade. [Allen 1977, pp. 56 and 73]

Virtually everyone Allen interviewed noted that there was seldom sufficient time to employ the sophisticated modelling techniques learned in graduate school and still meet the demands placed on practicing governmental economists.

The schism between upper-case Methodologists with their love of the Big Questions and the lower-case methodologists with their desire to be helpful is, I think, analogous to the schism that Allen observes. To be helpful to practicing model builders in economics, the grandiose methodological schemes that one might learn from reading the leading philosophers of science offer very little that can be applied to the practical methodological decisions that a model builder must make. Nevertheless, this schism too must be bridged and it is hoped that in what follows some progress will be made.

3. Applied methodology as a research programme

The chapters which follow represent a research programme that I began in the early 1960s. The programme was directed at bringing some commonplace notions to bear on some everyday methodolo-
gical decisions of practicing economists. When engaging in applied methodology it is important to keep things simple. While philosophers were still bickering over the intellectual merits of falsifiability of scientific theories, I set about seeing whether testability or falsifiability matters to the practicing economist who is actively building models. In the following chapters, I present the results of my research programme so far. After the initial chapter which argues that testability matters to both applied and pure theorists in economics, I present the foundation of my research programme which is an uncritical application of both the methodological requirement promoted by Paul Samuelson and the philo-
sophical demarcation developed by Karl Popper. My foundation is an operationalization of Popper's notion of degrees of testability. Chapters 2 and 3 show that rather ordinary modelling assumptions can lead to very different degrees of testability. In addition, I argue that if testability matters as much as most economic model builders

claim, it must be recognized that some modelling decisions increase testability while others make testability a *practical* impossibility. One might be tempted to ask whether the impossibility is due to broader issues than those of practicalities, but this question is postponed until Chapter 7. Instead, in Chapters 4 and 5, I ask whether testability is being used to conceal more important concerns such as the truth status of economic models.

As one must not throw the baby out with the bath water, I return to a consideration of how testability can matter to those of us who are still concerned with the truth status of economic models. In Chapter 6, I show how testability can be made an essential part of any informative equilibrium model. If one's purpose for building models of a behavioural theory is to test that theory then, in Chapter 7, I show that there are some substantial obstacles precluding successful tests. Does this mean that the methodological foundation of model building in modern economics is an impossible dream? Is it really impossible to test the truth status of economic theories by testing models of those theories? In Chapter 7 things may look bleak, but in Chapter 8 a way is found to make falsifiability a realistic methodological requirement for model building in modern economics. The book closes with some suggestions for those economists who wish to engage in their own research programme based on the study of economic methodology.

PART I

Applications of the
Popper-Samuelson Demarcation

1

Economic Understanding and Understanding Economics

Most sciences make a legitimate distinction between their *applied* and *pure* aspects, even though the borders are fuzzy.

Paul A. Samuelson [1962/66, p. 1668]

Mainstream neoclassical economists ... preach the importance of submitting theories to empirical test, but they rarely live up to their declared methodological canons. Analytical elegance, economy of theoretical means, and the widest possible scope obtained by ever more heroic simplification have been too often prized above predictability and significance for policy questions.

Mark Blaug [1980, p. 259]

The task of science is partly theoretical – *explanation* – and partly practical – *prediction and technical application.* I shall try to show that these two aims are, in a way, two different aspects of one and the same activity.

Karl R. Popper [1972, p. 349]

Today it is safe to say that most economists are concerned with practical problems and that they view the purpose of all economic theories as helping to solve these problems. It is not as safe to say (but it is equally true) that today most, if not all, economists are instrumentalists. That is, most are less concerned with the truth status of economic theories and more concerned with whether their theories produce useful results or predictions. This currently dominant methodological and philosophical bias in favour of practical problems and results can be most disconcerting for the large and ever-growing band of economic theorists who are often called 'pure theorists'. They are called 'pure theorists' because they (unfortunately) exclude the impurities of real-world complexities. Today we simply call them our 'theorists'.

Pure theorists are generally a hardy lot, hence we need not try to protect or defend them. There has been, however, a lot of needless controversy over certain methodological decisions which could have been avoided if we had been able to see that methodological controversies result from differences in purpose or that the objectives for many methodological decisions may be different. Given the prevailing bias regarding the purpose of theorizing and model building, it is quite difficult for the ordinary economist to see that the pure theorist is doing something quite different, and that his or her criterion for success may indeed be quite different.

The differences seem to be basically the following. Pure theorists are seeking to improve their *understanding* by creating new theories and models.[1] Having to assume something which leads to (one or more) false statements is totally unacceptable no matter how many true statements may validly follow. When they assume something which leads to statements which contradict known facts, they know that their bases for understanding (i.e. their assumptions) are, at best, inadequate. They would know that they do not really understand. Ordinary economic theorists – so-called 'applied theorists' – are seeking to solve practical problems. They attempt to create or modify theories and models to arrive at solutions to social problems or at specific policy directives. When they assume something, they would prefer to assume something which is known to be true, or 'approximately true', so as to guarantee that their conclusions are true or 'almost true' (assuming mistakes in logic are not made). Nevertheless, their operative criterion for acceptability of alternative assumptions is whether or not the assumptions lead to a (desirable) solution – the truth status of their assumptions is a secondary matter.

In this chapter I attempt to explain some of the methodological implications of this distinction in purposes, and particularly with respect to the question: Why do we assume what we assume? To assume one thing and not another is a methodological decision that

---

[1] If I take my TV set to an applied theorist (a TV repairman in this case), I do not question his understanding of electromagnetics – only his success at fixing my set. For all I know he may believe that there are little men in the transistors and thus he replaces transistors until he finds the 'culprit'. If he succeeds in finding and replacing the defective transistor, I can no longer distinguish his understanding of TV reception from that of any other repairman or even a modern electronics engineer.

all model builders and all theorists (pure or applied) have to make. And it is a decision which should always be open to criticism if we desire to learn anything at all about our understanding of economic phenomena and economic problems.

Throughout this book I am particularly concerned with the role of models in both the study of economic phenomena and the understanding of given economic theories. The former role centres on practical problems and the latter on what is usually called 'axiomatics'. The distinction in roles is made because the methodological decisions a model builder will make (with respect to particular assumptions) depend primarily on the purposes for which the model will be used. Given different purposes, our models may differ considerably with respect to such characteristics as generality and completeness. And a requirement (such as testability, simplicity and universality) of one model builder need not apply to another. Realizing the inapplicability of some requirements can help us understand many methodological controversies in economic theory and practice. However, identifying differences in purposes does not mean that the pure theorist can at last feel safe in his or her 'ivory tower'. At the end of this chapter I present an argument for how pure theorists, who may be concerned more with modelling theoretical ideas than with solving practical problems, can still be in touch with the real world of the applied theorists.

1. The role of models in economics

A theory is a *system* of ideas – or more specifically, a collection of systematically interrelated ideas. Theories, or systems, are necessary because individual ideas will not do the job, whether it be an intellectual job of understanding (or explanation) or a practical job of recommending an economic policy. Of course, an important intellectual job to be done is explanation, namely the explication of a particular answer to a particular question (or a solution to a problem). A typical practical job might be providing a solution to a practical problem and thus may require an adequate description of the circumstances of the problem.

The usual methodological controversy over whether theories are descriptive, explanatory, or predictive, and so on, stems from disagreements over the purposes, that is, the jobs to be done. So long as one is not looking for *the* purpose, there should be no controversy here. Theories created to do an intellectual job *may* be able to do a practical job. When applied economists are faced with a practical problem their task is to find a solution, or if they think they have a solution, they may wish to convince a policy-maker to employ their solution. One important source of solutions is the 'implications' of the various pure theories developed so far, thus the applied economist's task may become one of choosing between those theories.

Parenthetically, I should warn readers that economists too often use the terms 'implication' and 'logical consequence' interchangeably, even though this irritates some philosophers. A similar confusion is raised by the economists' use of the term 'tautology' when they really mean either a statement which is true by virtue of the definitions of its terms or any statement that is impossible to refute once certain conditions are accepted (e.g. the *ceteris paribus* condition) [see Boland 1981b]. While one might feel compelled to set economists straight on these distinctions, little is ever accomplished by trying to do so since these distinctions do not seem to matter relative to what economists intend to mean by their use. Nevertheless, whenever it is important to do so, I distinguish between how economists use these terms and their proper definitions.

What is the applied economists' criterion for choosing between theories? Is it the truth status of their theories? It need not be truth status unless the solution requires holistic, or very large-scale, changes [see Popper 1945/62]. The criterion need only be the success of a policy or solution implied by a theory. But, if there is no opportunity to try the policy or solution, an applied economist may rely on a comparison of the degrees to which the alternative theories have been 'confirmed' – i.e. on how much supporting evidence they have. Unfortunately, this criterion is not very reliable since it is not at all clear what is meant by 'confirmed' [see Agassi 1959, 1961; Popper 1965] and since the relative amount of supporting evidence can depend more on historical accident than the truth status of competing theories. Above all, whatever is meant by 'confirmed' it should never be used to defend against any criticism of a chosen policy since 'confirmed' never means verified (i.e. shown to be true). Obviously, if one of the alternative (pure) theories is true, it would be the theory to use, but of course we can rarely if ever prove a theory to be true because all theories involve universal statements (e.g. '*all* consumers are maximizers') which are by themselves not verifiable (no matter how much 'supporting' evidence we find) [see Popper 1959/61].

Most theories, and especially the individual ideas which constitute their ingredients, are non-specific with respect to formal relationships between the concepts involved in the ideas. For example, a theory may be based on the general idea of a downward sloping demand curve. We could assume an arbitrary curve, or be explicit and assume a particular shaped curve such as $\mathbf{P} = a + b\mathbf{Q}$ (where a and b are assumed to be fixed parameters) or even be more specific and assume, for example, $\mathbf{P} = 14.2 + 3.7\mathbf{Q}$. If our theories are in the form of explicit equations, then the policy implications of the theory can usually be made quite specific [cf. Brems 1959, Kuenne 1963]. Whenever one's theory is not explicitly stated, one way to determine if a theory is useful in a given practical situation is to build a 'model' of the theory much in the spirit of design engineering. For example, design engineers will often build a small model[2] of a new airplane design to test its aerodynamics in a wind tunnel. The design engineers – as applied theorists – will commit themselves to a specific model. Of course, many different models may be constructed (all based on the same new idea) by varying certain proportions, ingredients, and so on. Such opportunities for testing with scaled-down models seldom arise in economics. Thus when so-called 'applied economists' use a model, they should allow for error in a manner which will indicate the risk involved in being in error. One technique for such allowance is to use 'stochastic' models in which the possible error is explicitly represented in the model.

The word *stochastic* is based on the idea of a target and in particular on the pattern of hits around a target. The greater the distance a given unit of target area is from the centre of the target, the less frequent or dense will be the hits on that area. We might look at a model as a shot at the 'real-world' target. There are many reasons why we might miss the target, but they fall into two rough categories: (1) ours was a 'bad' shot, i.e. our model was false, and (2) the target unexpectedly moved, i.e. there is random *unexplained* variation in the objects we are attempting to explain (or use in our explanation). A stochastic model is one which systematically allows for the movements of the target. Stochastic models follow from a methodological decision *not* to attempt to explain anything *completely*. Non-stochastic models, by contrast, may attempt to

---

2 Here, I speak of a *small* model to distinguish it from a prototype model which is a *full-scale* working model.

give complete explanations. They do not allow for bad shots or moving targets.

To choose one approach over another involves a methodological decision. This decision is not open to theoretical criticism, but only methodological criticism. If our present theories are quite inadequate for practical purposes, then it might be wise to build stochastic models when we are interested only in practical usefulness. However, if we are interested in a *complete* understanding of phenomena, especially by improving on our present theories, building stochastic models may not be an appropriate strategy.

By constructing stochastic models, applied economists can try out various theories and compare them on the basis of the (potential) error (with respect to known data). The objective of the applied economist would be to use the policy implications of the model which minimizes the error (given the data at hand).

The applied economist assumes the truth of his or her model in order to apply it (see Chapter 3). The most common approach to dealing with the truth status of the model is to estimate the value of the parameters econometrically. In this approach one avoids specifying (a-priori) values for the parameters and uses actual data *ad hoc* to deduce the values of the parameters. The logically deduced values of the parameters are those of the hypothetical parameters of the posited model and are obtained only by assuming the model to be true (i.e. by assuming that together all the statements in the model form a true compound statement).

It must be stressed here that neither the applied economists' criterion of practical success nor their procedures will satisfy the pure theorists who routinely accept Karl Popper's philosophy of science. A false theory or model must surely be rejected regardless of how 'useful' it may be. If we do follow Popper in this manner, then in order to empirically criticize a theory we are required only to find one fact which is not compatible with that theory. Indeed, the existence of just one such fact indicates that at least one of the theory's assumptions is false. In other words, the discovery of even one fact which contradicts one of a theory's implications constitutes a refutation of that theory.

It might seem that non-stochastic *models* could play an important role in the empirical testing of theories which are not formally specific. However, does refuting a model of a theory necessarily constitute a refutation of that theory? The answer is clearly negative because in constructing a model we must add formal restrictive assumptions which are not necessary for the theory's job of explaining or justifying a conjecture. A model of a theory simply is not an implication of that theory, nor are the implications of a model necessarily identical to the implications of the theory it represents. To refute a theory using models requires that we show that *all* the possible models of a theory will be false.[3] It would seem that we have returned to Popper's requirement that we need to show at least one of the theory's implications to be false.

In the case of a theory which is explicit as to formal relationships – i.e. a theory which looks like a model – we could refute it by showing one of its solution statements[4] to be false. For the pure theorist who wishes to construct model-like theories to explain or demonstrate his or her conjectures it would be best to offer as many different (model-like) theories as possible (by varying the formal assumptions) in order to see the implications of the assumptions of particular forms of relationships. This, of course, would seemingly add to the intellectual efficiency since all the variations of the (model-like) theory could be tested simultaneously with the same data. But as with using models to test (more general) theories, the number of possible models (or in this case, possible variations of model-like theories) would be so enormous, and the individual models (or model-like theories) so specific, that we could expect them all to be false. If this is indeed the case – as we can be sure that it is – why do economists, including even some pure theorists, build model-like theories? For some it is a confusion as to methodological objectives – i.e. seeking solutions to theoretical problems vs seeking solutions to practical problems – but these economists can be excused for now. There are others who do understand the objectives of pure theory and still build model-like theories. And the reason clearly is that explicit models offer the opportunity to use a wealth of mathematical theorems. That is, by using mathematical theorems it is easier to show that a theory logically supports a particular conjecture. One of the methods of showing that a (model-like) theory does the job is to 'axiomatize' it

---

3 Note that this requirement is similar to the verification of a universal statement (e.g. 'all swans are white'); it is a logical impossibility (we would have to show this for *all* swans that currently exist, ever did exist, or ever will exist anywhere in the universe).

4 When we say a solution for a system of equations, we mean a set of values, one for each endogenous variable. I speak here of a statement of the value for one of these variables given the values of the necessary parameters and exogenous variables — that is the 'solution statement' for that endogenous variable.

and then demonstrate that it is consistent and complete – i.e. show that there exists a solution to the model and that the solution is unique. Being able to do a thorough and rigorous job in developing a theory is one of the advantages of building model-like theories.

2. On the foundations of economic ignorance: axiomatics

We assume when we don't know. The behavioural hypotheses upon which we build our economic theories are, so to speak, representations of our ignorance. Since the behavioural hypotheses are the foundation of our economic theories it seems reasonable to make them an object of study. One of the methods of studying the foundation of economic theory is called *axiomatics*. Before considering other uses for models, I will attempt to outline the nature of an axiomatic study and then discuss how model building may be a useful part of such a study.

Unfortunately, the only axiomatic studies completed so far have been by mathematicians and the more mathematically inclined economists – most notably Gerard Debreu, Kenneth Arrow, Abraham Wald and Tjalling Koopmans. Axiomatics as a distinct formal method has been around little more than 100 years. Originally it was concerned with the axioms and postulates of Euclid's geometry, and it is usually discussed in those terms. I shall attempt to refrain from that type of presentation here.

There has been little written expressly on axiomatics although little bits and pieces are to be found in advanced books on logic. It seems to be taken for granted that '[axiomatics] is a science in which we never know what we are talking about nor whether what we are saying is true' or that '[axiomatics] is the art of giving names to different things'. In all honesty one can say that its reputation comes from its being concerned only with form rather than substance and its deliberate attempt to create *systematic ambiguity*.

For the most part axiomatics is concerned with what are called 'primitive terms', 'primitive propositions' (postulates or axioms) which relate these primitive terms, and 'systems of postulates' (axiomatic systems). Axiomatics, then, is the study of the logical properties of such a system.

A system of postulates and primitive terms is analogous to a system of equations and variables. The problems associated with the properties of equation systems are similar to those which occur in axiomatics. When we solve a system of equations for X, we do so to answer the question: What determines the value of **X**? In axiomatics we might ask: On what basis can one logically derive the conclusion (or theorem) A? We might answer: (1) we can, using such-and-such axioms, or perhaps (2) given certain axioms, we cannot because the given system of axioms is either insufficient for such a derivation or involves a contradiction. Let us now look at some of the properties of axiomatic systems, namely the logical properties of consistency and completeness.

Consistency requires that the set of assumptions which make up a theory does not entail inconsistencies. As with systems of equations, a theory expressed as a system of axioms needs to be consistent, but with one important difference. Although a system of equations can be shown to be consistent, a system of axioms seldom can. However, a system of axioms can be shown to be inconsistent (as can a system of equations). This is an important consideration for the philosophy of science, since it is related to the difficulty of verifying a theory. To prove that a system is consistent it is necessary to show that *there does not exist* a statement for which both it and its denial can be deduced from the system.[5] To verify an explanatory theory (one which includes assumptions such as 'all consumers are maximizers') we must show that *there does not exist* a refutation, i.e. a false statement which is deducible from the theory. In each case, we may wish the positive but we can only prove the negative.

Consistency is obviously important since we cannot tolerate contradictions in explanations. For example, a theory which purports to explain resource allocations cannot imply that an economy at time *t* is both on and not on its production possibilities curve and be consistent. Consistency, however, does not rule out the possibility of a theory allowing for competing or contrary situations such as multiple equilibria. For example, all points on the production possibilities curve are potential equilibria differing only with regard to equilibrium price ratios. Any model which allows for flat spots on the production possibilities curve implies the possibility of more than one point being consistent with the same equilibrium price ratio.

Usually the question of consistency can be dealt with in a rather direct way by attempting to solve the system of equations

---

5 One proof of an *in*consistency would be the case where a contradiction is possible, that is, where both a given statement and its denial are logically allowed by the theory.

constituting the model of the theory. If an acceptable solution cannot always be obtained, it may be possible to specify additional conditions to guarantee a solution. Or, if non-acceptable solutions (e.g. negative prices or outputs) are logically possible, it may be possible to eliminate them by further specification, as is done when specifying that the marginal propensity to consume in the elementary Keynesian model must be between 0 and 1. Eliminating non-acceptable solutions is a low-order 'completeness criterion', i.e. the model must be complete enough to exclude them but it may not be complete enough to allow only one acceptable solution.

Completeness is the requirement that an explanation does not allow for the possibility of competing or contrary situations. As such it rules out the possibility of a false explanation accidentally appearing to be true. That is, if a theory or model is complete and happens to be false, we shall be able to show it to be false directly. For example, by assuming or demonstrating that the production possibilities curve has no flat spot and is concave, our explanation of the economy's output mix and equilibrium prices is complete since each point on the implied production possibilities curve is compatible with only one price ratio, and each price ratio is compatible with only one point on the curve. In other words, in a complete theory any possible equilibrium point is unique given any price ratio. Should any other equilibrium point be observed for the same price ratio, our theory would be refuted. Note that when we explain equilibrium prices we do not usually require the model to be complete with respect to absolute prices, but only with respect to relative prices. Completeness then is always relative to what we wish to explain. The conditions which assure consistency are usually much less restricting than those which assure completeness. For this reason, the question of completeness can be an important source of fundamental criticism. This is explored more fully in Chapter 6.

While consistency and completeness are the most important logical attributes of any axiomatic system, there are some second-order considerations: independence of axioms within a system, economy of thought, and the so-called 'weakness' of the individual assumptions. The secondary considerations are sometimes more interesting because they are associated with intellectual adventure, or are claimed to be matters of aesthetics.

Independence and Economy of Thought. Here again there is a similarity between systems of equations and systems of axioms. We can have a consistent system of (linear) equations where the number of unknowns is one less than the number of equations, so long as at least one of the equations is a linear combination of one or more of the others. Or there may be a subset of equations which does not involve all the variables of the system, thus indicating an independence between some of the variables. In an axiomatic system there may be dependence between some of the axioms such that one or more of the 'axioms' can be deduced from some of the others, or some of the axioms may use the primitive terms of another subset of axioms within the system. In the 'art' of axiomatics it is considered desirable to have axioms be independent so that none can be deduced from others. Independence of axioms is considered to be evidence of economy of thought.

Another aspect of economy of thought is the number of primitive terms and axioms. The elimination of axioms in order to minimize the number of axioms usually comes at a cost, namely increased complexity of the individual axioms. Obviously there is a limit to this.

Weakness of Axioms. Weakness has a lot to do with generality and universality, i.e. the list of things to be explained and the limits of applicability for the items on the list. It is considered desirable that the axioms be as 'weak' as possible. It is not always clear what is meant by this. It would seem that it has to do with how limited an assumption is in terms of the logical constraints placed on its primitive terms. For example, an assumption of a variable or quantity being non-negative would be said to be weaker than an assumption of its being positive since the latter would exclude more possibilities, in this case the possibility of its value being zero.

A successful axiomatic study of a theory should produce an effect similar to that of putting on a pair of new glasses having suffered myopia or astigmatism for a long time. The clarity resulting from understanding the logical structure of a theory offers opportunities to investigate the theory's truth status – ideally this is a concern of the pure theorist. An axiomatic study offers an opportunity to 'see' the basis of our understanding and thus is very useful in a systematic criticism of economic theory [cf. Morgenstern 1963]. By requiring us to present all the *necessary* assumptions (i.e. necessary for completeness) an axiomatic study enables us to reject *any* theory which requires as an assumption a statement which is *known* to be false. And if an axiomatic study shows a theory to be inconsistent or incomplete, then clearly this would be an important criticism of that theory.

Before a theory (or axiomatic system) can be completed it is usually necessary to show that it is incomplete. Most of the theoretical analyses in traditional textbooks can be interpreted as results (i.e. failures) of indirect attempts to show the traditional theory to be incomplete. Abraham Wald's famous study of the incompleteness of Walrasian general equilibrium is an example of an axiomatic study [Wald 1936/51]. An *incomplete* theory or axiomatic system (as a whole) may still be testable if it entails at least one testable statement. For example Samuelson offers an example of a testable statement from traditional consumer theory: the sum of compensated demand elasticities of each consumer for each good is zero.[6]

Wald's study offered to complete an axiomatic structure of his Walrasian model by adding extra assumptions. He added an *ad hoc* assumption that demand prices are always positive (his condition 5). Although the inclusion of Wald's additional restrictive assumptions does the job of completing *an* explanation of prices and outputs, it does not follow that they are *necessary* for the original theory. As was later shown, the existence and uniqueness of solutions of an entire Walrasian system can be achieved using linear programming or activity analysis models which do not require such restrictive assumptions. Thus it would seem that demonstrating that any one of Wald's conditions is not satisfied (in the 'real world') does not necessarily refute the original incomplete theory. I shall return to Wald's study in Chapter 6.

From the methodological position entailed in either Popper's philosophy of science or Samuelson's methodology, this state of affairs is rather perplexing. We may wish to complete an axiomatic version of traditional consumer theory and then criticize it. But if our criticism only deals with those assumptions or clauses which we add (or complete), then we are not really criticizing traditional consumer theory. It would seem that this can be overcome by attempting to deduce testable statements from the incomplete theory and submit these to tests. And if we show any one of them to be false, the theory *as a whole* will be shown to be false, no matter how it is eventually completed. This is a very

---

6 In Chapter 5 of his **Foundations of Economic Analysis**, Samuelson derives certain testable statements (such as the sum of a person's compensated demand elasticities for each good is zero) from assumptions which are not independently testable (e.g. *for every* person *there* exists a representable ordering on all goods) because the assumptions are of a logical form which does not permit falsification.

difficult task and not much has been accomplished so far. (We shall return to this in Chapters 7 and 8.)

From this methodological viewpoint it is important to realize that Samuelson's testable statement is deducible from a *set* of assumptions each of which is independently untestable, as will be discussed below. This being the case, we would conclude that it is certainly not *necessary* that the individual assumptions of our theories or models be testable in order to test the theory or model as a whole. Is the testability of each and every assumption even desirable? The answer is 'it depends'. For practical use of theories and models the answer may clearly be 'yes'. However, for purposes of intellectual adventure, economy of thought, aesthetics, etc., the answer may be 'no', since we may be more concerned with theories and models as *systems* of ideas [see Einstein and Infeld 1938/61, p. 30]. This question is considered again in the next section.

Having discussed economic models and economic theories, something needs to be said about what is called 'analysis'. What economists mean by analysis is not always obvious but it is possible to interpret their intentions. By recognizing explicit variables, a model builder is in effect analyzing the economic reality in question. An obvious example is the typical macro-economic equation, $Y = C + I + G$. Here the GNP is being analyzed into its components, C, I and G. Similarly, by expressing theoretical ideas in the form of a system of simultaneous equations, the economic system in question is being analyzed into separate ideas or behavioural assumptions – demand behaviour is represented by one equation and supply behaviour by another. In the context of axiomatics we can perhaps see more clearly the traditional role of analysis in the development of economic theory. In particular what is usually called 'theoretical analysis' in economics is the process of attempting to derive certain propositions, such as downward-sloping demand curves, upward-sloping supply curves, conditions of efficiency, of equilibrium, of maximization, etc., from a certain set of primitive assumptions. For example, given neoclassical consumer theory we might ask: Does our explanation of consumer behaviour, based on the idea of utility maximization facing a given income and given prices, entail *only* downward-sloping demand curves? An attempt to derive *upward*-sloping demand curves is, in effect, a test of the completeness and consistency of our given consumer theory (if it is to be used in a neoclassical price theory). In the case of indifference analysis, such an attempt succeeds if we do not rule out extremely inferior goods because then the possibility of upward-sloping demand curves arises. Specifically, the Hicksian assumption of a diminishing marginal rate of substitution along an indifference curve is insufficient for the avoidance of upward-sloping demand curves, although it is sufficient for consumer equilibrium! Unfortunately, exclusively downward-sloping demand curves may be *necessary* for the neoclassical theory of market prices [Boland 1977b, 1977d, 1986].[7]

One can see a positivistic bias in our traditional textbooks. Textbooks always seem to be telling us only about the propositions for which the traditional theory is sufficient. They seldom tell us anything about other relevant propositions for which the theory may be insufficient. If the traditional theoretical analysis is approached in a critical manner, it becomes a special case of axiomatic analysis. And if axiomatic analysis is approached in a critical way (by attempting to find important propositions for which the theory is incomplete), it can go a long way in helping to develop our economic theories, that is to say, our understanding of economic ideas and phenomena.

3. Beyond axiomatics

In the empirical social sciences, particularly economics, I think it is important that an axiomatic study also be concerned with the testability of the assumptions. This would at first seem to be an attempt to marry the two distinct approaches to economic theory discussed at the beginning of this chapter. However, I will suggest two different ways of considering the testability of assumptions. *Applied* theorists (or applied model builders) must be concerned with the testability of their assumptions. Preferably, their assumptions should be *directly testable*. On the other hand, the pure theorists or model builders who are interested in a model or theory as a *system* of ideas need only be concerned with the *indirect* testability of the assumptions – namely, in terms of the testability of the conjoint entailments.

The only time pure theorists require independent testability is when they find it necessary to augment their set of assumptions to

---

[7] That is, considering the arbitrariness of choosing between Marshallian or Walrasian stability conditions, only downward-sloping demand curves (and upward-sloping supply curves) will do the logical job of explaining market prices in *both cases*.

complete a model or theory. Any additional (*ad hoc*) assumption must be criticizable on its own because the additional assumption may make the model or theory true in a quasi-tautological manner. A theory can always be made true by assuming *ad hoc* that any conceivable counter-examples are exceptional cases not to be considered [see Hahn 1965b]. The question for the economist interested in learning about (or criticizing) his or her understanding of economic phenomena is always whether or not the unaugmented system of ideas (i.e. the model or theory) contradicts facts. Untestable *ad hoc* assumptions would only insulate the model or theory from the real world [see Boland 1974]. If the concern of pure theorists is their understanding (there does not seem to be any other that is exclusively their concern) which is manifested in the system of ideas (i.e. in their theory or model), then the individual ideas need not be their first concern.

For the sake of discussion, let us just say that pure theorists (as opposed to applied economists) are interested in models and theories as systems of ideas. In the process of building their models, theorists select assumptions. Should they select only assumptions which can be independently tested? In this section, I argue that from the perspective of pure theory, the objective in constructing models (or theories) will be to choose assumptions that are *independently untestable* and still do the job. It should be noted that this view is slightly weaker than the commonly accepted requirement (attributed to Hobbes [see Watkins 1965]) that we should choose only assumptions that are not known to be false.

Given the widespread adoption of the Popper-Samuelson view that testability is everything, many readers may find my argument in favour of independently untestable assumptions to be rather surprising. There certainly would seem to be many alternative objectives which would be more acceptable, such as postulating assumptions which: (1) are (necessarily) testable and, best of all, verifiable *if true*, (2) are tautological hence are always true, (3) are approximations of the real world, i.e. assumptions with a 'high probability of being true', or (4) may or may not be 'realistic' so long as they make the implications of a theory 'probably true'.

Each of these popular alternatives will be discussed in turn. I will try to show that each alternative methodological requirement (for model builders) has been based on a confusion of purposes or on a methodological error.

First I must explain what I mean by the phrase 'and still do the job' because it will play a prominent role in my arguments. I consider the job of an entire theory or model to be something more than just an exercise in (deductive) logic and by no means is it an exercise in 'inductive logic'. Theories are put forth in hopes of diminishing some of our ignorance.

Many economists believe that any theorizing is justifiable only to the extent to which its results are potentially useful [see Bronfenbrenner 1966]. They may be correct, but asking whether a theory will be potentially useful is superseded by the requirement of testability which in turn necessitates the requirement of falsifiability.

In economics we can go further in this logical chain. A falsifiable theory is not empirically testable unless it includes exogenous variables. This follows either from the avoidance of the identification problem or the desire for causal ordering [see Simon 1953]. However, the existence of exogenous variables in a theory immediately implies the potentiality of the theory being useful [p. 65]. But rather than just being useful in a practical sense (which may enhance our interest), the job of an entire theory is to help us to better comprehend phenomena and concepts (such as equilibrium [see Hahn 1973 on equilibrium theory]), i.e. to overcome the failures of our primitive comprehension of phenomena and concepts.

All theories can be characterized as attempts to 'justify' (i.e. to give reasons for) specific answers to specific questions. We assume what we assume in order to obtain our particular justification. The individual assumptions 'do the job' when they are logically sufficient for our justification! One of the purposes of *axiomatics* is to study their sufficiency and necessity for a particular justification. The *conjunction* of all the assumptions forms a specific representation of the ideas constituting the theory in question.

Taking a set of assumptions in conjunction permits us to deduce the implications of that theory. Now Popper's well-known falsifiability criterion requires only that at least one of these *implications* be (independently) falsifiable, but in no way does this requirement imply the necessity that any of the individual assumptions be independently falsifiable, let alone testable. Of course, following Hobbes, we realize that none of the assumptions should be known to be false! The task of deducing (testable) implications is merely an exercise in logic. Surely the job of the theorist is more than this. First, as indicated above, the theorist puts forth assumptions which do the job of establishing his or her desired justification (i.e. they are logically sufficient). There has been considerable controversy surrounding the question of whether all of the assumptions should be necessarily testable [see Boland 1979a]. If they were, and we could show any one of them to be false, any logical analysis of their implications (deduced from their conjunction) would be beside the point (and perhaps uninteresting) even if they are logically sufficient for their intended job! Should we be able to show all of them to be true, the job of the theorist degenerates to the somewhat more interesting job of being a practitioner of logic alone. Furthermore, if we were to require our assumptions to be tautologies (i.e. statements which are always true) then the theorist's job will clearly be only that of a logician. Thus, we can dismiss objectives (1) and (2), listed above, because they both reduce the job of the pure theorist to that of only a logician.

Now let us consider the alternative objectives (3) and (4) for the selection of assumptions (p. 31). Both of these objectives presume that we want our theories (i.e. their entailments) to be 'probably true'.[8] (Note well: this presumption implies an acceptance of a theory being 'probably false'!) Regarding the assumptions of our theories, advocates of these objectives can adopt a 'strong' view or a 'weak' view. *Excluding* followers of Friedman's instrumentalism [see Friedman 1953, as well as Boland 1979a], most economists believe in the strong view that as a theory's entailments should 'approximate reality' (i.e. be 'probably true') so should a theory's assumptions be 'probably true'. The concept of 'probably true' is represented by the probability of a statement being true where the means of determination is in accordance with one of several widely accepted conventional criteria such as minimum R^2. It is the conventionality of the criteria of truth status that gives this methodological view the title of 'conventionalism' (this is dealt with further in Chapters 4 and 5). The weak view, which may be ascribed to Friedman's followers, is that it does not matter if the assumptions are 'unrealistic' (i.e. 'probably false') so long as the entailments (i.e. predictions) are 'sufficiently accurate'. At times

---

8 There is the obvious difficulty for those of us who accept the axioms of ordinary Aristotelian logic: (1) a thing is itself (identity), (2) a statement cannot be *both* true and false (contradictions excluded), and (3) a statement can only be true or false (excluded middle). Together axioms (2) and (3) tells us that a statement either is true or it is false but not both. This also means there is nothing else it can be (such as 'probably true'). See further Swamy, Conway and von zur Muehlen [1985].

this weak view may suggest to some that there is a claimed virtue in the assumptions being false [Samuelson 1963]. It is this weak view to which Samuelson gives the name 'the F-twist' [see also Wong 1973].

Let us first look at the conventionalist (strong) view. Should we require that our assumptions be *approximations* of reality? That is, do we want our theories to be 'probably' true (and hence 'probably' false)? Here we reach a sensitive point with modern economists if we try to criticize the possibility of, or necessity of, the stochastic (or probabilistic) nature of economics. The difficulty in deciding this issue is due to the lack of a distinction between the objectives of the pure theorist and the objectives of the practitioner, namely the applied economist. The applied economist is primarily concerned with *success*, i.e. success in the practical job at hand (advising a government agency, a business, etc.). Surprisingly, the pure theorist is *not* concerned with success (at least not practical success). The pure theorist is more interested in what might be called 'intellectual adventure' [Agassi 1966b].[9] Unlike the applied economist, the pure theorist finds that he or she learns more from being wrong than from being right!

One important aspect of an intellectual adventure is the unexpectedness of the results, that is, on the basis of what we already accept (perhaps other theories) we should not expect a given new theory to be true. Now the traditional view is that if the assumptions were 'probably true', then the statements deduced from them may have a high probability of being true and therefore more useful [e.g. Bronfenbrenner 1966, p. 14], but this need not always be the case [see Boland 1982, Ch. 7]. Here again we find the job of the theorist reduced to that of a practitioner not of just logic, but of the logic of probability. There is a more fundamental problem with this view of the objectives of a theory and its assumptions. Do we (as theorists) want our theories to have an *ex ante* high probability of being true? If we are practitioners of economic theory, the answer is probably affirmative since success will be our criterion for evaluating a theory. From the viewpoint of the theorist interested in intellectual adventure it is more desirable for a theory to have unexpected results. That is, on the basis of what we already think we know (i.e. unrefuted previous theories), we would not expect the new theory to be true *and* if it were true

---

9 It might be called success in one sense — i.e. the success of creating a 'good' theory — but it is certainly not practical success.

then it would cast serious doubt upon the truth of our previous theories. A theorist could be more interested in a theory with a *low* rather than *high ex ante* probability of being true [see Popper 1959/61]. Thus 'pure' theorists would certainly not *require* their assumptions to have a high probability of being true.

Now let us look at the weak view. By saying that theorists do not *require* their assumptions to be true, or even have a high probability of being true, it is not intended to suggest that assumptions should be false! Obviously such a view would be ridiculous, as Samuelson has pointed out. This, I think, may be an unfair reading of Friedman's essay [see Boland 1979a]. Nevertheless we must be careful to avoid the possibility of this weak view being adopted. Whenever we require our assumptions to be only *probably* true (i.e. deemed to be true in accordance with some probability-based 'test conventions'), we must always leave open the possibility that the assumptions are false. If we were to have false assumptions then our understanding of the phenomena, or solution to the problem that the theory is supposed to justify, would surely be perverted [see Einstein 1950].

If a theory's assumptions are testable, then the possibility exists that we can (and should attempt to) show them to be false – or probably false in the case of stochastic theories (where 'probably false' means that the probability of being true is below a conventionally accepted minimum). If we are not interested in immediate practical usefulness, we can avoid this possibility by avoiding testability of our individual assumptions and let the burden of testability fall on the entailments of the theory as a whole. For example, the basic behavioural assumptions of traditional consumer theory may be axiomatically represented as follows:

(1)   for *every* consumer *there exists* some non-economic criterion *such that* he or she is able to compare combinations of quantities of goods;

(2)   for *every* consumer *there exists* an economic criterion *such that* he or she is able to compare combinations of quantities of goods;

(3)   every consumer when confronted by two combinations which he or she can afford, defined in assumption (2), will buy the one which is 'better', defined in assumption (1).

Assumptions (1) and (2) are not testable. They are both incomplete; the criteria are unspecified and thus none can be ruled out.[10]   Furthermore, assumption (3) is untestable because it depends on the other assumptions. The question here is whether the concept of 'better' is sufficient to be used to derive a testable statement from this theory. Samuelson specifically argued that it was sufficient to recognize that statement (3) presumes a choice is made and that the consumer is consistent in the application of the two criteria [see Samuelson 1938, 1947/65, 1950a].

We see then that the avoidance of individual (independent) testability amounts to saying that we make it impossible to know whether a *particular* assumption is true or false and leave it to be combined with other assumptions to form a theory. It is the theory as a *system* of ideas (rather than individual ideas or assumptions) which we are testing when we test a statement deduced from the conjunction of assumptions.

We can see another virtue of avoiding individual testability of assumptions and relying on the testability of systems of assumptions by considering another important aspect of an intellectual adventure, namely, the desire for economy of thought. If we accept Popper's classic means of demarcating scientific theories from non-scientific ones – i.e. the requirement of falsifiability [Popper 1959/61] – by requiring only that *at least one* statement derivable from a theory be falsifiable, then if we emphasize economy of thought in our development of a theory, we desire to *just* meet this requirement.[11]   Clearly, if any one of the derivable statements is already testable, then, in terms of economy of thought, we will go beyond the requirements if we also require that one or more of the theory's assumptions is *also* falsifiable on its own.

It might be well and good to say that, from the standpoint of 'pure' theory (i.e. of systems of ideas) and of intellectual adventure, it is desirable to avoid individual testability of assumptions. It is quite another matter to show that it is possible to have individual

---

[10] Statements of this form are sometimes called 'all-and-some statements' and as such are incomplete. One can complete them. The completed statement may be falsifiable but it is not a necessary outcome [see Watkins 1957].

[11] However, emphasizing economy of thought in this sense would seem to run counter to Popper's criterion for deciding which of two compatible theories is 'better', namely that the theory which is 'better' is more testable. But the testability of a theory is dependent more on the testability of any of its implications than on the number of implications. The testability of any of its implications is inversely related to the quantity of information, i.e. the 'dimension of a theory', required to test an implication. This topic is examined more fully in Chapters 2 and 3.

assumptions untestable and still have at least one of the statements derivable from their conjunction (i.e. the theory formed by them) testable. But as noted above in my axiomatic example of consumer theory, Samuelson seems to have done this already (see the example above as well as his [1947/65, Ch. 5]). This means that it is indeed possible to satisfy Popper's criterion of refutability (a criterion which assures us of the possibility of empirically criticizing a theory) and still be concerned only with the theory or model as a system of ideas rather than empirical truths (i.e. 'realistic' assumptions).

As an axiomatic study, my version of traditional consumer theory is incomplete for two reasons: (1) it lists only the behavioural hypotheses, and (2) each individual assumption, as a member of a conjunctive set, is not complete with respect to the specification of necessary presuppositions and limitations entailed in the assertion that the assumptions *together* do the job of justifying the given answer to the given question. In particular, since all the assumptions for the behaviour of consumers are of the form of quantificationally incomplete statements, the metatheoretical assertion that they do the job requires that to complete the theory, we specify the necessary and sufficient conditions of maximization [see Boland 1981b]. What we can (or must) specify for a particular assumption depends on what the other assumptions say – i.e. it is a 'simultaneous argument' similar to a system of 'simultaneous equations'. In this manner traditional consumer analysis can be thought of as attempts to complete these clauses.

4. Testability for all

The title of this chapter indicates a distinction between two approaches to the study of economics. This distinction has implications for the methodological decisions involved in developing a theory or model. In particular, this distinction implies differences in the criteria of success of a model or theory, in the purposes for model building and in the epistemological requirements for the assumptions used in a model or theory.

Ideally there would be no need to distinguish between understanding economic phenomena and understanding economics. However, until we know all there is to know about economic phenomena, the distinction remains important. The intention is not to try to build a philosophical wall around either applied economists or pure theorists, but by recognizing the existence and the incompatibility of these two alternative approaches, to make it possible for more fertile criticism between them.

The models we build represent our understanding of specified economic phenomena. The individual assumptions of our models or theories form the foundation of our understanding. The implications of our models can be important for two different reasons. The implications can be useful (policy recommendations, etc.) and they can be a means of testing our understanding. Clearly, our understanding can be open to criticism. But if it is beyond direct criticism, either because the applied economist has chosen assumptions which appear to be realistic or because the pure theorist may have designed assumptions that are individually untestable so as to emphasize the model as a system, then we must rely on indirect criticism by testing the implications. So long as the implications are testable and none of the assumptions are known to be false, we need not be afraid of the pure theorist's apparent disinterest in the realism of his or her assumptions. But these are important conditions of acceptance. Axiomatic studies must take testability into consideration. And if we really are interested in understanding our economic understanding, we must reject methodological statements that suggest our assumptions can be allowed to be false.

So-called 'pure theorists' cannot insulate themselves by hiding behind a wall of aesthetics and scholasticism. They must put their systems of ideas to test and the only convincing test is against the 'real world'. Of course, here the applied economists can help a great deal, but they must attempt to appreciate what the pure theorist is attempting to do if the theorists are ever going to listen to their criticisms.

Similarly, applied economists should not be deluded by limited practical success or 'positive' results. Pure theorists may be able to offer useful criticism but they should not ignore the importance of practical success. If pure theorists wish to criticize an apparently successful model, they will never convince anyone until they also explain why that model is (or appears to be) successful.

2

On the Methodology of Economic Model Building

To be of interest a scientific theory must have consequences. Upon hard-boiled examination, the theory of
consumer's behaviour turns out not to be completely
without interest. By this I mean: consumption theory does
definitely have some refutable empirical implications.
The prosaic deductive task of the economic theorist is to
discern and state the consequences of economic theories.

> Paul A. Samuelson [1953, p. 1]

the *refutability* or *falsifiability* of a theoretical system
should be taken as the criterion of its demarcation.
According to this view, ... a system is to be considered as
scientific only if it makes assertions which may clash with
observations; and a system is, in fact tested by attempts to
produce such clashes, that is to say by attempts to refute
it.... There are, moreover, *degrees of testability*, some
theories expose themselves to possible refutations more
boldly than others.

> Karl R. Popper [1965, p. 256]

It would seem that the most important statement deduced from a
multi-equation economic model is its solution. The solution
statement specifies a certain relationship between that which we
wish to explain (the endogenous variables) and that which we
know (or assume to know) or can be independently determined (the
parameters or the exogenous variables). The main concern of this
chapter is the significance of the epistemological problem which is
associated with the truth status of the *form* of an economic model.
Unless we *know* in fact the values of the parameters, the solution is
nothing more than a conditional statement. Nevertheless, we can

compare models (and the theories they represent) by comparing the forms of their solution statements.

1. Economic theories and the aim of science

The purpose of this chapter is to present the quantitative criterion of testability by which the forms of the different models can be compared. This criterion was developed in my 1965 PhD thesis [Boland 1966]. To develop this criterion I chose to depart from what I thought at the time was the typical philosophical viewpoint about the purpose of science and economic theories. The alternative which I chose is a version of what I now call the 'Popper-Socrates view of science' [Boland 1982, Ch. 10]. I did not consider just *any* alternative view but one which seemed to offer an opportunity to ask what appeared to be some new or different questions about the truth status of economic models.

Let us begin by presenting this alleged alternative view of science. After developing some useful concepts which follow from this view, I will illustrate them with some examples of simple economic models. In this context, the most important concept I develop is Popper's 'dimension of a theory'. Simply stated that is the number of observations *necessary* to refute a theory or model [cf. Samuelson 1947-8, pp. 88-90]. With this concept in mind, a few models will be compared on the basis of their different dimensions.

1.1. Science as an unending process

In the remainder of this introductory section, I present the view which in 1965 I wished to attribute to economic model builders. My view then was that economists as scientists do not seek theories which are 'true statements' or even 'almost true statements'. Thus I presumed that anyone who envisages a system of absolute, certain, irrevocably true statements, or 'probably' true statements, as the end-purpose of science would certainly reject the alternate view of science I used in my PhD thesis. To appreciate the Popper-Socrates view of science, consider the purpose for which we advance theories in economics. My view in 1965 was that science is not a singular act, i.e. an act of advancing just one theory – if it were, we would probably wish that each singular theory be put forth as a 'true statement'. To the contrary, with the alternate view of science as a guide, I claimed that science is an endless succession of revision, i.e. the replacement of an inferior theory with a less inferior theory which in turn is replaced by a slightly less inferior theory, and so on. Methodologically speaking, such a process must begin somewhere. So following Popper, I said that it begins with a conjecture, an attempt at explanation of some phenomena. However, this conjecture would *not* be offered as a (known) true statement but as something on which we may begin to make improvements. Thus I claimed that we advance theories because we need something to improve. Moreover, if we see science as a process of making advances, not only will the statement or conjecture which we offer not be a (known) true statement, but to get things going we may even need to begin with a false statement.[1]

As this may seem rather perverse to some readers, let us consider a few reasons. Most students of epistemology or methodology seem to assume (implicitly or explicitly) that there is something which might be called True Knowledge and that it is a *finite* quantity, although the process of obtaining it may be unending [see Boland 1982, Ch. 4]. Of course, one can attempt to describe or explain large or small portions of this quantity. Because it is claimed to be a finite quantity, some epistemologists and methodologists behave as if the Archimedes Principle[2] applies – they seem to think that by advancing theories which are in a small part true, there exists the possibility of a *finite* number of theories which when combined will describe Reality, i.e. add up to that finite maximum of knowledge, True Knowledge. Today, as in my 1965 thesis, I reject this view of knowledge because the conception of knowledge as a finite quantity represents a methodological bias in favour of inductivism [see Boland 1982, Ch. 1]. In its place, I will presume that truth status is a quality, i.e. all non-paradoxical statements must possess the quality or property that *either* they are true *or* they are false [see Boland 1979a]. Knowledge is *not* like wealth, since if it were, we would always try to obtain *more* of it.

---

[1] After more than twenty years this seems rather naive to me. In later work I realized that many would interpret 'known true' to mean 'tautologically true' and thus see that all that was being required was the potentiality of being false rather than the naive claim that advances imply false conjectures.

[2] The Archimedes Principle says that if there is a finite positive quantity A and there is a positive quantity B such that $B < A$, then there exists a finite number n such that $nB > A$.

Knowledge is more like health, to the extent that we can always try to *improve* it.[3]

With regard to economics and for the purposes of this chapter, I will treat Reality or the True World at any point of time as a 'Walrasian-like' system of an unknown number of equations (or a very large number for which there is always the possibility of adding more) and an indefinite number of unknowns [cf. Georgescu-Roegen 1971]. Economists, however, operate with the expectation that over time there are some salient features of this system which do not change very much, if at all [see also Hicks 1979, Ch. 4]. But here, too, economists do not expect to be able, *a priori*, to describe these features exactly, although one can expect to be able to show when a feature changes.

1.2. The Popper-Socrates view of science

The Popper-Socrates view of science shall be described as follows: Science begins by attempting to overcome certain inabilities to explain some unexpected phenomena (e.g. certain features of the economic system such as the capital stock and the level of GNP, which apparently change together) or it can begin with a mythological statement (e.g. the lack of a balanced budget is bad for the country) or it can begin with a statement of theory about some empirically observable phenomena (perhaps phenomena not yet observed, such as a predicted recession next year). Theories are advanced in order to overcome some real or conceptual problems in explanation. The starting point will not matter – so long as each succeeding theory presents new problems which must be overcome, i.e. new problems for which new theories are offered to solve the succeeding problems, inabilities or difficulties. If the new theories do not present new problems, the process would cease. Thus if science is to move along, we as theorists must seek new problems. And to do this we advance theories which we may perversely hope will be false, even though we offer them as potentially true theories.[4] The idea that a new theory should be

---

3 And even if one were to have 'perfect knowledge', one would have to strive to maintain it (like perfect health) by countering any attempts to put forth false statements. Nevertheless, we need not pursue this analogy any further.

4 Of course, hardly anyone *expects* to find absolutely correct theories – e.g. a theory which would perfectly explain the year 1988. But it must be realized such a theory which does not is, 'as a whole', a false theory even though certain subparts of it may be true [see Samuelson 1964].

able to explain some new phenomena is secondary to the survival of any science. Showing a new theory to be in some additional regard false gives us an important prize, namely a new problem to be explained or overcome. The necessity of a new theory's ability to explain what a previous theory can explain is, so to speak, a necessary but *not* sufficient condition for it to be an interesting new theory.

When one implication or conclusion of a theory (or model) is shown to be false, then clearly the theory *as a whole* is false. Thus in these strict terms it would have to be concluded that most (if not all) economic theories are false. Nevertheless, we as economists do not discard all of our theories. This is mainly because we do not have a 'better' theory with which to replace the false theories, although there may be many candidates [see Archibald 1966]. Applied theorists are concerned with the applicability or workability, but not necessarily the truth status [see Boland 1979a], of any theory which they wish *to use*. Some theories are better than others, or more than one theory will do the job required. In the absence of straightforward practical tests, how do 'pure theorists' decide when one theory is 'better' than the other?

The criterion with which theories are compared follows from one's prior view of the aim or purpose of science. With the Popper-Socrates view of science as a guide, any science may be considered a social activity and as such it needs some guidelines or 'rules'. However, these rules may merely be conventions rather than rules such as those of logic. The Popper-Socrates view prescribes rules in order that everyone can participate. Certainly more is accomplished by a team than by a group of individuals operating each with his or her own private conventions. A set of rules can make the social activity easier and more interesting but cannot assure success or even 'progress' (whatever this means). Any rules which are proposed must not be arbitrary, rather they must follow *logically* from the aims which are attributed to any science.

The Popper-Socrates view says that we conjecture hypothetical solutions or theories in order to attempt to improve them, which means that we may wish theories to be false to some extent. That is to say, there must be something to improve. However, when we put forth a theory we do not *know* that it is false – i.e. that any of its conclusions will be false. We only learn that a theory is false after we have tested it and have shown that it has not passed the test. Thus, if the discovery of errors or failures depends on the ability of our theories to be shown false, we can logically accept the property of falsifiability as one of our criteria. Of two competing and unrefuted theories, the one which is more falsifiable is considered to be 'better' to the extent that it is worth being the first to try to refute. On this basis, one can argue for the absolute requirement that, to be of scientific interest from the Popper-Socrates perspective, any suggested solutions to new problems (or answers to new questions) be in principle falsifiable or refutable.

1.3. Theory comparison and the dimension of a theory

In Section 2, an explicit argument for today's commonplace absolute criterion of falsifiability will be based on two reasons: (1) there is no point in discussing what economists call tautological theories since nothing can be learned with them, and (2) since the objective is to produce theories in order to criticize them, the theories must be capable of being false. In other words, only theories which are falsifiable or refutable are useful within the Popper-Socrates view of science. I stress that falsifiability is necessary but *not* sufficient for the purpose of science which I have attributed to Popper. The requirement of falsifiability is thus not sufficient for the description of the Popper-Socrates view of science. To put things in a broader perspective, it might be noted that there have been some methodologists who viewed science as the pursuit of true theories (although some may qualify the pursuit to be towards approximately true theories). According to this so-called 'verificationist' view, we present theories in order to verify them, which requires that theories be verifiable [see Machlup 1955]. However, verificationists may still require falsifiability since it would be trivial to verify tautologies. Falsifiability is necessary for *both* the Popper-Socrates view of science and the old-fashioned 'verificationist' view which Popper criticizes. (I will have more to say about this irony in Chapter 7.)

An additional criterion will be discussed by which a selection can be made between competing theories, i.e. those theories which explain the same phenomena. This criterion will involve two related properties of theories: degrees of falsifiability and degrees of testability.[5] Whenever there are two theories which explain the

---

[5] For now we may define these as the relative quantity of conceivably falsifiable statements, and quantity of empirical statements, respectively, which can be deduced from a theory.

same phenomena (i.e. the same list of endogenous variables) or produce the same solution to the same problem, the more interesting theory is the one which is relatively 'more falsifiable'. If the competing theories are apparently of equal or incomparable falsifiability, then the more interesting theory is the one which is relatively 'more testable'. The degree of testability will be shown to depend on what Popper calls the 'dimension' of a theory, such that the lower the dimension, the higher the testability.

Popper's choice of the word 'dimension' may seem unfortunate because I will use it in the comparison of infinite sets. Let me, then, briefly digress to explain how I will be using the word dimension in a rather formal sense. For my purposes, the dimension of a set is *the dimension of its boundaries plus one* – e.g. the dimension of a cube is three (although it may contain an unlimited number of 'points') since the boundaries of a cube are squares which in turn have the dimension two. Likewise, a square has the dimension of two because it is bounded by unidimensional lines which are in turn bounded by points which have dimension zero. Although one may claim there are an infinity of points within the boundaries of the set defining a cube, the set has a finite dimension. (For a more rigorous discussion of this notion of dimension, see [Hurewicz and Wallman 1948].)

1.4. Science as a community activity

To investigate the 'real world' of a Walrasian-like system in small but *definite* steps can be incredibly difficult. Thus to make any reasonable advance one might choose to be methodologically efficient. It can be suggested that one means of being efficient is to offer as many solutions as possible when attempting to overcome a failure of a previous theory. Only after a reasonably complete list of possible solutions is obtained does the use of the criteria of falsifiability or testability begin. Unfortunately only when theories which cannot be eliminated by these criteria remain will it be necessary to devise new criteria such as 'crucial' tests or pragmatic simplicity. The smaller the steps or the improvements, the easier the compilation of possible solutions, i.e. the more manageable will be the task of science.

Since the Popper-Socrates view stresses the conception of science as a community activity rather than a private activity, the need for succinct presentation would seem almost crucial. Community efforts will appear to be best served if one explicitly spells out: (1) the problems (or questions) which a theory claims to solve (or answer), (2) the solution (or answers), (3) the means (arguments, models, assumptions, etc.) by which a particular solution (or answer) is to be derived, and (4) how one might attempt to refute the remaining theory or decide between the remaining theories. However, none of these guidelines guarantee anything.

This then is the Popper-Socrates view of science as I understood it in the 1960s. In the remainder of this chapter I will present my attempt to apply this view to some of the elementary methodological tasks of economic model building. Of special interest are those aspects of the Popper-Socrates view which will help in the comparison of the forms of various economic theories. My 1965 analysis began with a discussion of the so-called 'problem of demarcation', i.e. the alleged problem of distinguishing between scientific and non-scientific statements. This discussion was essential for anyone wishing to use Popper's philosophy of science, even though it is easy to see that such considerations are not necessary [see Bartley 1968]. While I think it is necessary to discuss Popper's demarcation criterion in order to discuss his more useful idea of the dimension of a theory, I must stress here that I am not interested in developing methodological rules or criteria which would restrict the freedom of economic theorists to ask certain questions. Rather, I am interested only in comparing the quality or *forms* of the theories and their representative models against a background that specifies the aim an economist has for his or her science.

2. Popper's famous demarcation criterion

Since it is commonly thought that the keystone of the Popper-Socrates view of science is its *requirement* of falsifiability of all truly scientific statements, the first task would seem to be a consideration of the implications of a demarcation between scientific and non-scientific statements [see Hutchison 1960]. Falsifiability is definitely the hallmark of many popular discussions of the relevance of Popper's philosophy of science for economic methodology [e.g. Blaug 1980, Caldwell 1982]. For Popper, a falsifiable statement is important because the truth of a falsifiable statement implies a prohibition of the truth of other statements. Although in many, but not all, cases statements may be both falsifiable and verifiable, for the purposes of the Popper-Socrates view of science, falsifiability is preferred to verifiability. This preference is established to exclude certain statements or questions from consideration on the basis that nothing can be learned from a statement or an answer to a question if that statement or answer cannot be wrong. Statements or answers to questions must be such that they can, in principle, be falsified.

Despite the efforts of many of us to credit Popper with revolutionizing economic methodology by his emphasis on falsifiability, it is only fair to recognize that falsifiability has long been the basis of Paul Samuelson's methodology [e.g. Samuelson 1947/65]. However, Samuelson does not explain why he is interested in falsifiable statements (which he calls 'operationally meaningful'). Consequently, the following discussion of what I will call the 'Popper-Samuelson demarcation' will have to be based only on Popper's explanations of what I have called the Popper-Socrates view of science.

2.1. Falsifiability vs verifiability

Let us review some of Popper's fundamental distinctions. First, falsifiability does not always imply verifiability. A statement such as 'all swans are white' can, in principle, easily be falsified, but it can never be verified since we must look at all swans that ever did or ever will exist. Similarly, the statement 'there exists at least one white swan' can easily be verified, but it can never be falsified because we would have to show that *every* swan that ever did or ever will exist is not white. Popper calls a statement such as the first, which uses the unlimited concept 'all', a *strictly universal* statement; and he calls a statement such as the second, which uses some form of 'there exists', a *strictly existential* statement [Popper 1959/61, p. 68]. Clearly the negation of a strictly universal statement is equivalent to a strictly existential statement and vice versa. Thus it can be said that the falsifiability of a theory is its ability to be used to deduce strictly universal or *non-existential* statements [p. 69]. In other words, a theory is falsifiable if one can deduce from it statements which prohibit certain conceivable phenomena. For example, one may deduce from a theory that the interest rate is non-negative (i.e. $i \geq 0$) or one may deduce that the rate of change of GNP with respect to time is always positive (i.e. $\partial GNP/\partial t > 0$).

The establishment of falsifiability as an operative demarcation criterion directly excludes existential statements and tautologies.

Tautologies are excluded because they are always true and thus can *never* be falsified. Emphasis on falsifiability also assures that self-contradictory statements will be excluded since they can be shown to be false by *any* observation or test. An example of a self-contradictory statement would be 'the interest rate is non-negative *and* the interest rate is negative'. The observation of a positive or zero interest rate would indicate that the second half of the statement is false while a negative interest rate would indicate that the first part is false. Since the interest rate is a real number the statement is *always* false, and hence will always be rejected [p. 91].

If the operative demarcation criterion were verifiability rather than falsifiability, tautologies would not be excluded necessarily since they can be easily verified. Also if we *only* looked for verification when testing statements or theories, the self-contradictory statement runs the minor risk of not being quickly eliminated. Of course it is easy to see the contradiction in our example, but when the contradiction is much more subtle or complex we run such a risk. The point here is that the concept of falsifiability is more convenient since the same restrictions are possible with the concept of verifiability *only* if it is *also* specified that tautologies and self-contradictory statements must be excluded from consideration. The difference between a demarcation using falsifiability and a demarcation using verifiability will be diminished somewhat since the Popper-Socrates view of science also requires that theories under consideration must be consistent [p. 75]. The importance of the requirement of consistency will be appreciated if it is realized that a self-contradictory (prohibitive) statement is uninformative. A consistent (prohibitive) statement divides the set of all possible observations or statements of fact into two groups: those which it contradicts and those with which it is compatible [p. 92]. I postpone discussion of 'informativeness' until Chapter 6.

2.2. *Falsifiability vs false theories*

If it is kept in mind that a theory or model consists of many assumptions which are logically conjoined to form an argument in favour of one or more propositions, we must now consider what the Popper-Socrates view of science means by a 'false theory'. If statement P follows logically from theory T and if P is false then the theory T *as a whole* is false. But it cannot be inferred that any one assumption used in the theory is, or is not, specifically upset by the falsification. Only if statement P is independent of some part T' (or group of assumptions) used by theory T can it be said that the part T' is not involved in the falsification. The problem of ambiguity of falsifications with regard to assumptions will be discussed further in Chapters 7 and 8.

Sometimes it appears to be possible to alter the theory slightly and eliminate the offending false implication. For example, let us say we have deduced from a growth model the following relation:

$$Y_n = g(n, Y_0) \qquad [2.1]$$

where Y_n is the GNP of the nth period following period 0, $g()$ is a function involving the parameters of the model and Y_0 is the GNP for period 0 (i.e. for $n = 0$). Also, let us say we know what g and Y_0 actually are and we have 'tested' the model by observing GNP for various periods and have found that the calculated Y_n did not agree with the observed Y_n; specifically, the actual GNP was always greater than Y_n by an amount equal to a constant multiple of n (i.e. by kn). We might consider adding to our model an 'auxiliary hypothesis' that actual GNP $= Y_n + kn$. Such attempts are not unusual in the natural sciences [Popper 1959/61, p. 88]. Consider another type of modification. Let us say that our observation indicated that the solution represented by equation [2.1] was true after period 10. We can 'salvage' our model in this case by adding the restriction that [2.1] holds for $n > 10$. Either of these modifications (a transformation or a restriction) can 'save' a model, but only at the expense of its simplicity or generality. The Popper-Socrates view of science rules out such modifications on the basis that they are in conflict with the aims of a purely theoretical science [Popper 1959/61, pp. 82-3]. This does not mean that all auxiliary hypotheses should be rejected [see Boland 1974]. For example, consider the following solution deduced from a simple Keynesian model:

$$Y = K/(1 - b) \qquad [2.2]$$

where Y is GNP, K is the level of investment, and b is the well-known 'marginal propensity to consume'. If the simple model under consideration only specified that b is not zero, very little would be prohibited by equation [2.2] – i.e. the equation [2.2] is compatible with many different Y/K ratios. An auxiliary hypothesis which says that b is positive but less than one would, in this case, improve the model by making it more susceptible to falsification. In general, with the exception of theories which have been modified by an auxiliary hypothesis which makes them easier to falsify, modified theories will be considered to be inferior to unmodified theories.

2.3. *Consequences of using the Popper-Samuelson demarcation*

On the basis of the demarcation criterion prescribed by both Popper and Samuelson, we can draw some conclusions about what type of theories or enquiries are prohibited. The demarcation based on falsifiability and non-falsifiability divides possible theories into two groups: (1) those theories from which non-tautological, non-universal prohibitive statements can be deduced, and (2) those theories from which either strictly existential statements or tautological statements or both can be deduced. Not much more can be said about the first group until a concept of 'degrees of falsifiability' is specified (this is our task in the following section).

The second group includes two types of statements which most scientists have little difficulty excluding from science. Falsifiability, however, offers something more than an intuitive basis for excluding them. As indicated, the two important members of this excluded group are: (a) tautological statements, and (b) strictly existential statements. We exclude both direct tautological enquiries (e.g. concerning statements that are true by virtue of their logical form alone – such as 'I am here or I am not here') and statements deduced from systems consisting of only definitional statements. Statements deduced from systems of definitions are quite common in mathematics (in fact this is one way to characterize pure mathematics). Economic theories, however, are based on more than definitions and tautological statements. Economic theories must always include one or more behavioural assumptions or conjectures, i.e. they must run the risk of falsely interpreting the behaviour in the 'real world'.

The second type of excluded statement, the existential statement, seldom occurs in the literature of modern economics. When it does, it is most often in the form of a prophetic statement. For example, consider a prediction or conclusion that there will be a social revolution. We can never refute such a claim because when we note that the revolution did not occur, its proponents will always say that it is still in the future.

Before concluding the discussion of Popper's idea of demarcation, one other requirement placed on the theorist should be noted. The demarcation based on falsifiability also leads to the requirement that economists who attempt to 'measure' capital, output, rates of return, capital coefficients, etc., must always specify the theory in which the particular concept of capital, or output, etc., appears. Without knowing the theory, one cannot know whether or not the economist's efforts only involve tautologies, hence one cannot *know* what will be learned by such a measurement [see Briefs 1960].

In the remainder of this chapter it will be assumed that the Popper-Samuelson demarcation criterion of falsifiability has been applied so that any remaining questions will be about comparisons or evaluations of falsifiable theories or models. Some falsifiable theories can be shown to be 'better' than others if we can measure a theory's 'degree' of falsifiability or testability.

3. Popper's subclass relations and the comparison of theories

Having now eliminated the 'unscientific' statements and theories by using the demarcation based on falsifiability, economic model builders need a criterion by which they can compare statements or theories that remain. For this purpose, Popper offers a criterion which logically follows from the Popper-Samuelson demarcation – namely, the concept of 'degrees of falsifiability' [Popper 1959/61, Ch. 6]. With this concept one theory can be judged 'better' than another on the basis that one theory is '*more* falsifiable' than another.

To understand the concept of degrees of falsifiability, one must understand the properties of a falsifiable theory or statement. According to Popper's view of science, a theory is falsifiable if it rules out certain 'possible occurrences' [p. 88]. A theory is falsified if any of these possible occurrences actually occur. To avoid possible semantic difficulties with the word 'occurrence' Popper chose to speak of the truth or falsity of the statement that a particular event has occurred or can occur [pp. 88-91]. He called such a statement a 'basic statement'.

At that time, Popper was attempting to explain his view of science in terms that would appeal to the reigning analytical philosophers [see Bartley 1968]. Therefore, he offered to provide an analysis of the falsifiability of a given theory by *analyzing* all the possible basic statements that can be deduced from the theory. To classify the basic statements that can possibly be deduced from a theory, following Popper, let P_a, P_b, P_c, ..., represent elements of a class (or set) of occurrences which differ *only* in respect to individuals involved (i.e. to spatio-temporal locations or subclasses when they refer to similar things, for instance consumer goods). Popper called this class 'the event (P)' [Popper 1959/61, pp. 88-91].[6] To illustrate, one may speak of 'the event (prices of consumer goods)' where members of this class may include the price of apples (P_a), the price of butter (P_b), the price of coffee (P_c), etc. In Popper's terminology, the statement 'P_c is one dollar per kilogram' is called a 'singular statement' which represents the class 'the event (price of consumer goods)'. The singular statement 'P_c is one dollar per kilogram' asserts the occurrence of 'the event (price of consumer goods)' for coffee.

All singular basic statements which belong to one set or class of events (e.g. the relative prices for all consumer goods) will be called 'homotypic'. The singular statements which are homotypic *but* differ only in regard to their syntax (hence are logically equivalent) and thus describe the same event, will be called 'equivalent'. Although singular statements represent particular occurrences (i.e. particular observation statements), universal statements *exclude* particular occurrences. For example, the universal statement '*all* prices of consumer goods are positive' excludes the occurrence of negative or zero prices of all consumer goods.

Now in terms of this semi-formal framework we can say that a theory is falsifiable if and only if it always rules out, or prohibits, *at least one event*. Consequently, the *class* (or set) of all prohibited basic statements (i.e. potential falsifiers of the theory) will always be non-empty.

To visualize this Popperian notion of basic statements, imagine a horizontal line segment which represents the set of all possible basic statements – i.e. something like the totality of all possible economic worlds of economic experience. Let us further imagine that each event, or class, is represented by a subsegment, a 'slice', of our horizontal line segment. Now let all the homotypic statements which belong to a particular class be 'stacked' vertically like tiles (in any order) on our horizontal subsegment which represents

6 Unfortunately the term 'event' may seem a little vague when applied to economic concepts but this is because we are seldom succinct in our identification of economic variables. If we were to follow the suggestions of Koopmans or Debreu, we would have to say 'price of coffee *at place* A and *at time* T'. Thus our economic variables would appear to be more compatible with Popper's discussion of the concept of events.

that class (e.g. the price of a consumer good). Finally and to complete the picture, let us place in a segment of the horizontal plane all the basic statements (tiles) which are (logically) equivalent to one particular homotypic statement and let them be distributed directly behind and in the same vertical slice as that homotypic statement, thereby forming a wall of tiles. Thus the totality of all possible statements about economic events can be described by a three-dimensional space. In terms of this picture, the idea of falsifiability can be illustrated by the requirement that for every 'scientific' theory, there must be *at least one* vertical slice of a positive thickness in our diagrammatic space which the theory *forbids*. Similarly, for theories which are tautological there does not exist such a slice, and for theories which are self-contradictory the slice is the whole space.

Now the 'space' envisaged here consists of only Popperian basic statements. Before comparing various slices of this space which are prohibited by different theories, I will define more specifically what is meant by a 'basic statement' [Popper 1959/61, p. 100]. The statements which are included in the 'space' must satisfy the following two conditions if they are to be relevant for the demarcation criterion of falsifiability: (1) no basic statement can be deduced from a universal statement *without* initial conditions or parametric values, but (2) a universal statement and a basic statement can contradict each other. Together conditions (1) and (2) imply that a Popperian basic statement must have a logical form such that its negation cannot be a basic statement [p. 101]. In Section 2 of this chapter I discussed Popper's well-known view of statements with different logical forms, namely universal and existential statements. It was noted that the negation of a (strictly) universal statement is always equivalent to a (strictly) existential statement and vice versa. To speak of the occurrence of a single event is to speak of the truth of a singular basic statement (or singular non-existential statement). This suggests the following rule regarding basic statements: Basic statements (i.e. tiles in our imagined picture) have the logical form of singular existential statements. Singular existential statements differ from strictly existential statements in that the former is more specific. For example, where a strictly existential statement would be 'there are positive profits', a singular existential statement would be 'there are positive profits in the coffee industry'. Consider one more requirement which is less formal: The event which is the subject of a basic statement must be, in principle, an observable event. In short, basic statements are observation statements.

.Comparison of the falsifiability of two theories amounts to the comparison of two sets of classes of falsifiers (statements which if true would contradict the theory). In terms of our imagined picture of the world of economic experience, this means the comparison of slices of the 'space' of possible occurrences. Ideally, one would like to have a concept of measure or a concept of cardinality (or power) of a class. Unfortunately, such concepts are not applicable because the set of all statements of a language is not necessarily a metric space.

A concept which will work in some situations is the subclass (or subset) relation [pp. 115-16]. Consider two theories: theory *A* which is falsified by statements in slice [*a*] and theory *B* which is falsified by statements in slice [*b*]. In this regard three situations can be identified:

(1) If and only if the slice [*a*] includes *all* of slice [*b*], i.e. slice [*b*] is a proper subclass (or subset) of slice [*a*], then theory *A* is said to be 'falsifiable in a higher degree' than theory *B*.

(2) If the slices are identical (i.e. the classes of potential falsifiers of the two theories are identical) then they have 'the same degree of falsifiability'.

(3) If neither of the classes of potential falsifiers of the two theories includes the other as a proper subclass (or subset), i.e. neither slice contains all of the other, then the two theories have 'non-comparable degrees of falsifiability'.

In situation (1) the subclass relation would be decisive, in situation (2) it is of little help, and in situation (3) it is inapplicable.

In the following section, we shall be primarily concerned with situations (2) and (3). Ideally, all methodological questions about 'theory choice' [e.g. Tarascio and Caldwell, 1979] would be reduced to cases of situation (1), since all other criteria are not as decisive as the subclass relation (see further Chapter 5). To close this section, let us consider a rather simple example of the comparison of two theories (specifically, two models representing the theories) that can be based on the concept of the subclass relation. Consider the following variables:

Y ≡ GNP, i.e. aggregate spending,

C ≡ the portion of output demanded for use as consumer goods,

K ≡ the portion of output demanded for use as new capital goods,

R ≡ the interest rate.

For the purposes of this simple example, the comparison is between competing theories which differ only in regard to the list of endogenous variables.

Model 1

$$Y = C + K \qquad\qquad [2.3]$$
$$C = a + bY \qquad\qquad [2.4]$$
$$K = k \qquad\qquad [2.5]$$

where a, b and k are parameters.

Model 2

$$Y = C + K \qquad\qquad [2.6]$$
$$C = a + bY \qquad\qquad [2.7]$$
$$K = d/R \qquad\qquad [2.8]$$
$$R = r \qquad\qquad [2.9]$$

where a, b, d and r are parameters.

Statements about **Y**, **C**, and **K** can be deduced from the model of the first theory and about **Y**, **C**, **K** and **R** from the model of the second theory. Thus the comparison between these theories satisfies the ideal conditions and, using Popper's views, it can be concluded that the second theory (Model 2) is 'more falsifiable' than the first theory (Model 1). Note well, this does not mean that it is *easier* to falsify, i.e. that it is more testable! In any case, such ideal situations are not very interesting. In the following section I will undertake the task of describing the determinants of the 'size' of the slice for a theory, especially in situations which are not ideal, namely situations (2) and (3). A more general discussion of theory-choice criteria will be postponed until Chapter 5.

4. Testability and Popper's dimension of a theory

In this section, I discuss some important methodological objectives and concepts which are compatible with the Popper-Samuelson demarcation criterion of falsifiability. Of most interest is the determination of how each can help in the comparison of the 'slices' of different theories when they do not fit the ideal situation. Unfortunately, there has been very little study of the mechanics of comparing economic theories so I shall borrow language from higher mathematical analysis because the concepts are intuitively similar. The most important concept to be developed is Popper's 'dimension of a theory'.

Let us consider some common concepts about theoretical statements and how they are related to falsifiability. Since the elements of the 'space' described in Section 3 were statements about occurrences, or better, observation statements, it is safe to conclude that these are empirical statements derivable from the theory in question. The class (or set) of potential falsifiers (i.e. our 'slice') may be called the 'empirical content' of the theory in question, such that empirical content is less than or equal to the 'logical content' (the class of all non-tautological statements derivable from the theory) [Popper 1959/61, pp. 113 and 120]. Since logical content is directly related to falsifiability, Popper says that empirical content is directly related to 'testability' [p. 121]. A theory which is easier to falsify is 'better testable'. Since what determines a theory's *success* is its ability to *withstand* severe 'tests', we will be concerned with the empirical content. When the empirical content of a theory is increased (i.e. the 'size' of the slice is increased), Popper says that it is made more testable and hence more falsifiable [pp. 119-21]. Stated this way, Popper's view may imply a misleading connection between testability and falsifiability. The distinction will be easier to discuss after we have considered some explicit economic models. For the purposes of this chapter, it will not be necessary to distinguish between falsifiability and testability with respect to the Popper-Socrates view of science.

Consider what Popper seems to think determines the empirical content and hence falsifiability of theories and statements. Popper notes that there are two common methodological objectives which may be reduced to the demand for the highest possible empirical content, namely the demand for the highest attainable 'level of universality', and the demand for the highest attainable 'degree of precision' [pp. 121-3]. Let us examine the following conceivable 'economic laws':

P: the time-path of the output of *all* goods can be described
by a segment of a circle (i.e. by an equation of the *form*:
$t^2 + y^2 + Et + Fy + G = 0$).

Q: the time-path of the output of *all agricultural* goods can be described by a segment of a circle.

R: the time-path of the output of all goods can be described by a segment of a conic (i.e. by an equation of the *form*: $At^2 + By^2 + Dty + Et + Fy + G = 0$).

S: the time-path of *all agricultural* goods can be described by a segment of a conic.

According to Popper, the deducibility relations holding between these four statements are as follows: From P all others follow; from Q follows S, which also follows from R; thus S follows from all the others.

Moving from P to Q the 'degree of universality' decreases. And Q says less than P because the time-paths of agricultural goods form a proper subclass of the time-paths of all goods. Consequently, P is more easily falsified than Q: if Q is falsified, then P is falsified, but *not* vice versa. Moving from P to R the 'degree of precision' (of the predicate) decreases: circles are a proper subclass of conics. And if R is falsified, then P is falsified, but, again, *not* vice versa. Corresponding considerations apply to the other moves: If we move from P to S then both the level of universality and the degree of precision decrease; from R to S the level of universality decreases; and from Q to S the degree of precision decreases. A higher degree of precision *or* level of universality corresponds to a greater (logical or) empirical content, and thus a higher degree of falsifiability.

On the basis of the desirability of universality and precision, Popper establishes the following rule: 'If of two statements both their universality *and* their precision are comparable, then the less universal or the less precise is derivable from the more universal or more precise; unless, of course, the one is more universal and the other more precise' [p. 123]. According to Popper, this rule demands that we leave nothing unexplained – i.e. that we always try to deduce statements from others of higher universality. He says that this follows from the fact that the demand for universality and precision can be reduced to the demand, or rule, that preference should be given to those theories which can be most severely tested.

This then is the foundation for a Popperian view of theory choice: choose the theory with the maximum degree of falsifiability (more precision, more universality, or both). Let us now see how Popper developed a concept of dimension which is associated with the testability of a theory. Generally the subclass relation will not be directly applicable to the comparison of economic theories and models. A quantitative criterion is needed which is not possible with such class or set concepts. As stated in Section 3, the set of falsifiers (our 'slice') includes all 'basic statements' which, if true, would falsify (i.e. contradict) the theory in question. It was also noted that Popper's basic statement is an observation statement, so let us now ask: What is the composition of an observation statement? Popper says that they are composed of '*relatively* atomic statements' (such as observed magnitudes for the variables or parameters of the theory) [p. 128]. They are 'relative' because where or how one might make these observations in order to test the theory must be specified. A set or class of such relatively atomic statements can be defined by means of a 'generating matrix' (e.g. the data published by the federal Department of Agriculture for the last ten years). The set of all these statements together with all the logical conjunctions which can be formed from them may be called a 'field'. A conjunction of N different relatively atomic statements of a field may be called an 'N-tuple of the field'. For this 'N-tuple' Popper says that its 'degree of composition' is equal to the number N [p. 129].

Consider a theory A, where there exists a field F of singular (although not necessarily basic) observation statements and there is some number D such that the theory A can never be falsified by a D-tuple of the field F, but it can be falsified by some $D+1$-tuple, then we call D the 'characteristic number' of the theory relative to field F. According to Popper, the class of all singular statements in this field F whose degree of composition is less than or equal to D, is then compatible with (i.e. permitted by) the theory regardless of their content [p. 129].

Since any singular statement (e.g. the list of all current prices for agricultural products) may be included in the field, it is possible to encounter difficulties and inconsistencies if some of these statements are irrelevant for the theory in question. Therefore, Popper spoke only of the 'field of application' for a theory. A rough idea of the concept of a 'field of application' is the list of variables and parameters of a model.

Now I can describe a basis for comparison of testability of theories which is associated with the characteristic number of a theory and will define what I call the *Popper-dimension* of a theory T with respect to the field of application F. A theory T will be called '*D*-dimensional' with respect to *F* if and only if the following relation holds between *T* and *F*: there is a number *D*, the Popper-dimension of theory *T* with respect to field *F*, such that the theory does not clash with any *D*-tuple of the field [pp. 285-6]. The concept of a field was not restricted to basic statements, but by comparing the 'dimensions' of the singular statements included in the field of application, the degree of composition of the basic statements can be estimated. According to Popper, it can thus be 'assumed that to a theory of higher [Popper] dimension, there corresponds a class of basic statements of higher dimension, such that all statements of this class are permitted by the theory, irrespective of what they assert' [pp. 129-30]. The class of permitted statements is the 'complementary set' with respect to the slice which was described in Section 3 – i.e. they are the complementary set with respect to the field of application.

Now, I shall illustrate the concept of the Popper-dimension with the statements Q and S (discussed at the beginning of this section) using some notions borrowed from elementary analytical geometry. The hypothesis Q – that the time-path of the output of *all* agricultural products is of the form: $t^2 + y^2 + Et + Fy + G = 0$ – is three-dimensional. This means that, if this statement is false, its *falsification* requires at least four singular statements of the field, corresponding to four points of its graphic representation. Likewise, hypothesis S – that the time-path of the output of *all* agricultural goods is of the form: $At^2 + By^2 + Dty + Et + Fy + G = 0$ – is five-dimensional, since at least six singular statements are necessary for falsification, also corresponding to six points of its graphic representation.

At the beginning of this section it was possible to conclude that Q is more falsifiable than S because circles are only special cases of an ellipse or a conic (viz. an ellipse with eccentricity zero). That is, circles are a proper subclass of the class of all ellipses and the class of all conics. Note, however, a circle is *not* a special case of a parabola (for which the eccentricity is always equal to 1). Thus the subclass relation cannot be used to conclude that the hypothesis Q is more falsifiable than an alternative hypothesis S′ which differs from S by asserting that time-paths are parabolic. However using the concept of a Popper-dimension as the operative criterion, it can be correctly concluded that Q is more falsifiable than S′. Since a parabola is four-dimensional at least five singular statements are needed for the falsification of S′. Note also that the dimension of a set of curves depends on the number of *coefficients* which are free to be chosen. For example, a general second degree curve is algebraically expressed as: $Ax^2 + By^2 + Cxy + Dx + Ey + F = 0$. Setting the coefficients $A = B$ and $C = 0$, and eliminating two coefficients, yields the general equation for a circle. Setting *only* $4AB = C^2$ eliminates another coefficient and thereby yields the general equation for a parabola. In the case of a circle, only three coefficients are left to be freely chosen. For a parabola, only four coefficients are free. Thus Popper says that the number of freely determinable coefficients of a set of curves (or time-paths as in our example) by which a theory is represented is characteristic for the degree of testability of that theory [p. 131].

The concept of dimensions of curves can be extended to surfaces. This is convenient since the solution (specifically the parametric equations which describe the solutions) of a model can be generally described as a surface. Consider the following simple model.

Model 3

$$Y = C + k \qquad\qquad [2.10]$$
$$C = bY \qquad\qquad [2.11]$$

where Y and C are endogenous variables and k and b are considered to be exogenous parametric variables.

Since we do not *know* that b is the same for all observations, we must allow for all possible values. Hence we must treat b as if it were a variable. The solution of this model is:

$$Y = k/(1 - b) \qquad\qquad [2.12]$$
$$C = bk/(1 - b) \qquad\qquad [2.13]$$

Let us illustrate the concept of the Popper-dimension by considering equation [2.12]. This is a second-degree equation or more properly, it is *at least* a second-degree equation. Since we do not *know* that it is higher, for convenience sake, I will choose the lowest possible case. Expressing a relationship between all the possible values of Y, k and b (the unknowns) yields a general equation of the following form:

$$AY^2 + Bk^2 + Db^2 + Ekb + FYb + GYk + HY + Jk + Lb + M = 0 \quad [2.14]$$

Rearranging equation [2.12] yields:

$$k - Y + Yb = 0 \qquad\qquad [2.12a]$$

If in equation [2.14] we let $J = 1$, $H = -1$, and $F = 1$, using [2.12a] we can reduce equation [2.14] to:[7]

$$AY^2 + Bk^2 + Db^2 + Ekb + GYk + Lb + M = 0 \qquad [2.15]$$

For equation [2.15], six coefficients are free to be chosen. Thus the Popper-dimension of this model is six since it would take at least seven observations (non-coplanar points in the graphical space) in order to falsify this model. Equation [2.12] can be interpreted to say that the solution of the model asserts that the relationship between the endogenous variables and what are considered to be the exogenous variables forms a special case of a second-degree surface, namely one which also satisfies [2.12a]. I am concerned here only with the formal aspects of a model's solution, thus whenever [2.12a] holds [2.15] must hold as well. From a methodological point of view it would be helpful to consider all parameters, such as b in [2.11], as unlimited exogenous *variables* whenever their values (or the limits of their values) are not actually *known*.

Consider Model 2 (discussed in Section 3) with respect to the solution for Y (i.e. GNP) – its Popper-dimension is 51 (as I will show in Chapter 3). This may seem to be a rather large dimension for such a small model. Clearly it might seem to some that the higher the Popper-dimension, the greater the risk of the theory becoming virtually tautological [see Popper 1959/61, p. 127]. Perhaps we should consider ways to reduce the dimension of a theory. The most common method is to specify initial conditions.

In effect, the specification of initial conditions is the requirement that the 'solution surface' passes through particular points of the graphical space. In this sense, every set of initial conditions reduces the Popper-dimension by *at least* one. An example of an initial condition would be to require that in our statement Q above, the time-path pass through the origin of the graph.

The Popper-dimension of a theory or statement can be reduced in another way. For example, in statement Q, circles in general may be changed to circles with a given curvature. The change reduces the dimensions of statement Q by one since its falsification would now only require three observation statements. Popper calls this

---

[7] This method is only an approximation. A more involved but more accurate method is to consider the relationships between the coefficients under all possible translation or rotation transformations. This would help to eliminate some of the free coefficients and thus reduce the estimate of the Popper-dimension.

method of reduction (i.e. of changing the form of the curve) a 'formal reduction' of the dimension of Q. He calls the other method (i.e. of specifying initial conditions) a 'material reduction' of the dimension of Q [p. 133]. Both methods have a similar effect on the algebraic representation of the statement – namely both determine one of the coefficients thus leaving us with one less coefficient which we may freely choose.

Note that two statements may be of equal dimensions. For example, if our statement R must hold for two sets of observations (i.e. certain outputs at two points in time), the dimension of R is reduced to three, which is also the dimension of statement P. However, statements P and R are not equivalent since statement R still allows for conical paths and statement P only circular paths. Thus it can be said that R is still more 'general' than P, in that a circle is a special case of a conic.

In economics we are usually interested in unique solutions of models – that is, given a set of values for all the parameters and exogenous variables, there is only one set of values for the endogenous variables. If there were more than one set of values for the endogenous variables which would not contradict a model, it might be said that the model in question is 'more general' than a model with a unique solution. If the values of all the parameters and exogenous variables were known then generality might be desirable. Since in this chapter such knowledge is being excluded, a criterion such as 'generality' will be disregarded. In other words, I am noting here that generality and what might be called 'specificity' are not necessarily opposites. A specific hyperbola hypothesis is no more 'general' than a specific straight-line hypothesis if both can be refuted with one observation.

The concept of a Popper-dimension will be illustrated in Chapter 3. The idea of reducing the dimension of a theory can play an important role in economic model building. I will, however, have to be more careful than Popper was about applying these concepts. The solution of an economic model is a set of parametric equations – i.e. a set of equations each of which expresses one endogenous variable as a function of parameters or exogenous variables. In the illustration using Model 3, only the dimension of one of these parametric equations or statements was discussed. If Popper's criterion is extended, it must be concluded that the Popper-dimension of an entire theory (assuming there are no separable independent parts) is the minimum dimension of all the possible parametric solution statements. In Model 3, it so happens that the

Popper-dimension of both parametric equations, namely equations [2.12] and [2.13], were the same. In general this will not be the case. For example, in Model 2, the minimum dimension is 7. This extension is possible because, as Popper says, on the basis of *modus tollens*, if one statement P is shown to be false, then the theory *as a whole*, which was required for the deduction of P, is falsified [see Popper 1959/61, p. 76].

3

Implementing the Popper-Samuelson Demarcation in Economics

> Every genuine *test* of a theory is an attempt to falsify it, or to refute it.
>
> Karl R. Popper [1965, p. 36]

In the construction of an economic model the model builder must make methodological decisions about the following: (1) what variables are to be included in the models, (2) which of these variables are to be specified as exogenously determined, and (3) what should be the form of the relationship between the exogenous and endogenous variables. Throughout this book I am concerned with the formal 'benefits and costs' of every aspect of decisions concerning the construction of models in economics. From the standpoint of 'benefits' one would expect that: (a) the larger the number of variables included, the better, (b) the greater the proportion of endogenous variables (i.e. variables to be explained by the model) over exogenous variables, the better, and (c) the more complex (less linear) the form of the relationships, the better. These expectations are held because one suspects that this is the way the 'real world' is. These factors, or attributes, are then the formal 'benefits' of the model constructed. Unfortunately, the increase in any one of these factors, or attributes, usually comes at a 'cost', namely, a decrease in the testability of the model constructed.

Why do some economists consider a reduction of testability a cost? For some optimistic proponents of the Popper-Socrates view of science, 'progress' in science is precluded if we fail to replace theories which have been shown to be false (and/or inadequate) with 'better' theories. New theories must explain why the old theories went wrong as well as what the old could explain. For these proponents of the optimistic Popper-Socrates view, true science is a progressive sequence of models [e.g. Koopmans 1957, Weintraub 1985].

If a new theory or model is constructed in a manner that makes it logically difficult to test (e.g. it has a very high Popper-dimension or it is a tautology), then one reduces the chances for progress by reducing the necessity of replacing it, i.e. by reducing the appearance of failures. In one sense then the reduction in testability is a long-run cost. By a reduction in testability I mean an increase in the Popper-dimension which results from the particular methodological decisions of the model construction discussed above. An increase in Popper-dimension by virtue of a new model (or theory) is then an increase in the long-run theoretical cost of a particular set of methodological decisions (e.g. the cost of changing from a linear model to a non-linear model).

In the short run – that is for the purposes of immediate practical use of the economic theories or models – one may not be as concerned about the testability or even the general truth status of one's models so long as they do their intended practical job. For the applied economic theorists, the question of the model's truth status is not immediately important. However, it may become important should the model or theory fail to assist in the practical job!

1. Calculating the Popper-dimension of explicit models

In light of my discussion of the Popper-Socrates view of science and the implementation of the Popper-Samuelson demarcation criterion expressed in degrees of falsifiability (i.e. the Popper-dimension), I now examine a few specific economic models, some of which can be found in the literature. What will be most interesting is the rather high Popper-dimension of rather small models. In most cases I consider the determinants of the Popper-dimension and how the dimension can be reduced in hopes of making the models more falsifiable. It must be stressed here that I am concerned with the *form* of the solution of a model, thus I will treat all solutions as if we do not know the actual values of the parameters. This amounts to treating the parameters as exogenous *variables*. I will examine the 'methodological sensitivity' of all the parameters and forms of relations. For the eleven simple models used as illustrations, it will be found that the Popper-dimension varies from a low of zero to a high of over 475,000.

Let us begin with a simple macro model from the end of Chapter 2. As with all models discussed there, I will use bold capital letters for the endogenous variables and lower case letters for both parameters and exogenous variables. Initially, I consider only the following variables to be endogenous:

$$\mathbf{Y} \equiv \text{GNP or aggregate spending,}$$
$$\mathbf{C} \equiv \text{aggregate consumption.}$$

Model 3

$$\mathbf{Y} = \mathbf{C} + k \qquad [3.1]$$
$$\mathbf{C} = b\mathbf{Y} \qquad [3.2]$$

where k and b are considered exogenous.

The solution of this model is:

$$\mathbf{Y} = k/(1-b) \qquad [3.3]$$
$$\mathbf{C} = bk/(1-b) \qquad [3.4]$$

Equation [3.3] may be rewritten as:

$$\mathbf{Y} - b\mathbf{Y} - k = 0 \qquad [3.3a]$$

I shall now interpret [3.3a] to be a special case of a second-degree surface in 3-space – i.e. a special case of:

$$\Phi(\mathbf{Y},b,k) = 0 \qquad [3.3b]$$

In general, the algebraic representation of our second-degree surface in 3-space is:

$$0 = A\mathbf{Y}2 + Bb2 + Dk2 + Ebk + F\mathbf{Y}k + G\mathbf{Y}b + H\mathbf{Y} + Jb + Lk + M \qquad [3.5]$$

where non-bold capital letters denote coefficients. Note that in general there are nine free coefficients. We are not free to select the value of the tenth coefficient because, except for a special case, that would lead to a contradiction. By *not* specifying the tenth coefficient we are describing a family or system of equations (or surfaces) of a particular *form* – rather than *one* particular equation of a particular form. The emphasis here is with the form. For example, we may be interested in the truth status of *any* linear model not just the truth status of *one* specific linear model.

Considering equation [3.3a], if we let G=−1, H=1, and L=−1, we are left with the following:

$$0 = AY^2 + Bb^2 + Dk^2 + Ebk + FYk + Jb + M \qquad [3.6]$$

Again, I wish to focus attention on the *form* of the solution and in particular on the question of whether or not the surface [3.3b] (or [3.5]) describes the solution of the model. I stress that I am concerned only with a methodological problem: Can a second-degree surface be found that is compatible with [3.3a], i.e. a surface which satisfies both [3.3a] and [3.6]? Since there are six free coefficients, it should be easy to find such a surface. Thus the Popper-dimension of this model is six because it is not *necessarily* compatible with *any* seven coefficients. Specifically, it would take a basic statement consisting of seven observations of **Y** *and* **C** in order to refute the solution – each observation yields a b and a k which must satisfy both [3.1] and [3.2] as well as [3.6] such that:

$$0 = \mathbf{Y}^2 A + (\mathbf{Y/C})^2 B + (\mathbf{Y}-\mathbf{C})^2 D +$$
$$(\mathbf{Y/C})(\mathbf{Y}-\mathbf{C})E + \mathbf{Y}(\mathbf{Y}-\mathbf{C})F + (\mathbf{Y/C})J + M$$

In other words, although it may be possible to find coefficients of equation [3.6] which render [3.6] compatible with six observations or points, it is not *necessarily* possible to find a second-degree surface which will 'pass through' any arbitrary seven 'points' [see also Samuelson 1947-8, pp. 88-90].

In this example, the Popper-dimension can be determined by observing the general form of the surface because the number of terms are relatively few and the surface is in only 3-space. In general, the Popper-dimension of a solution equation depends on three properties of that equation: its degree, the number of unknowns implicit in it, and the number of terms in it. If we let the degree be δ and the number of unknowns be ω (hence our surface is in 'ω-space'), we can determine the number of terms, N, that would be free to be chosen in the complete general form equation of the solution surface as follows:

$$N + 1 = (\delta+1)(\delta+2)(\delta+3)...(\delta+\omega) / \omega! \qquad [3.7]$$

or in symbolic notation:

$$N + 1 = \Sigma_1 \Sigma_2 \Sigma_3 ... \Sigma_\omega r \qquad [3.7a]$$

where the summation Σ is over $r=1$ to $r=\delta+1$. This is a generalization which follows by means of mathematical induction such that letting $\omega=1$ yields:

$$0 = A_1 + A_2 x^1 + A_3 x^2 + ... + A_{\delta+1} x^\delta$$

When $\omega = 1$ the list of indices will be the following series: $(1,2,3,4,5,\ldots,\delta+1)$. And letting $\omega = 2$ will yield the following:

$$
\begin{aligned}
0 = {} & A_1 + \\
& A_2 x_1 + A_3 x_2 + \\
& A_4 x_1 x_2 + A_5 x_1^2 + A_6 x_2^2 + \\
& A_7 x_1^2 x_2 + A_8 x_1 x_2^2 + A_9 x_1^3 + A_{10} x_2^3 + \\
& A_{11} x_1^3 x_2 + \ldots \qquad\qquad + A_{15} x_2^4 + \\
& \text{etc.}
\end{aligned}
$$

Note here that the list of the indices for the last coefficient in each line is the following series (1,3,6,10,15, etc.). Also note that each term of this series can be further analysed: $1 = 1$, $3 = 1+2$; $6 = 1+2+3$; $10 = 1+2+3+4$; $15 = 1+2+3+4+5$; or generally, $\Sigma_1 \Sigma_2 r$. Thus by mathematical induction, equation [3.7a] can be obtained.

1.1. More testable is not always more falsifiable

It could be inductively concluded that [3.7a] is equivalent to [3.7] by substituting various values for δ and ω and obtaining the same values for N [see Salmon 1928, Woods 1961]. This possibility raises two problems that require some adjustment to the concept of the Popper-dimension of a theory if it is going to be applied to specific economic models.

First, if we let the number of terms given by the solution equation be t then the Popper-dimension equals $(N-t)$. This consideration requires no adjustment since it seems to correspond to what Popper had in mind when he compared the testability of circles and conics as noted in Chapter 2. To illustrate, consider Model 3 (p. 66). The degree of [3.3a] is 2. The number of unknowns in [3.3a] is 3 hence the model is in 3-space and the number of terms given in [3.3a] is 3. Thus using [3.7] yields:

$$N + 1 = (2+1)(2+2)(2+3)/(1 \times 2 \times 3) = 10 = 9 + 1$$

Therefore $N = 9$, but the Popper-dimension of Model 3 with respect to **Y** is 6, i.e. $(9-3)$. Note that the Popper-dimension of Model 3 with respect to **C** is also 6.

Second, by expressing Popper's idea of the field of application as being the list of parameters and variables, we see how Popper's view that equates the degree of testability and the degree of falsifiability may lead to apparent contradictions. In Chapter 2, I noted that a theory which explained more variables was, in Popper's eyes, more falsifiable because it was more at risk of being refuted. Here I am saying that since it raises the Popper-dimension of the theory, more variables means less testable. Actually by more variables Popper was referring to a greater domain of application for the same list of variables, such as going from prices of all agricultural products to prices of all products. Here we are talking about changing the list of variables and we are concerned with the practicalities of defining a successful test. Since in economics we are typically not concerned with the question of a domain of application for a variable, rather than entering into a technical argument over whether my definition of a Popper-dimension of a theory accurately represents what Popper had in mind, I will henceforth call it the 'P-dimension'. Here it will always be the case that the testability of an explicit model goes down (because the P-dimension goes up) whenever the number of variables or the maximum degree of the equations increases *ceteris paribus*. Whether a more testable explicit model is necessarily more falsifiable will not be a concern here since the question of more or less testability better represents the methodological concern of modern economists who define a successful test as a refutation (e.g. Samuelson and the followers of his methodology).

1.2. The P-dimension as a measure of testability

Now consider Model 1, previously discussed in Chapter 2 (p. 55), which differs from Model 3 in that the former includes 'autonomous consumption'.

Model 1:

$$\mathbf{Y} = \mathbf{C} + k \qquad\qquad [3.8]$$
$$\mathbf{C} = a + b\mathbf{Y} \qquad\qquad [3.9]$$

where a, b, and k are considered exogenous variables.

First, let us determine this model's P-dimension. The solution for $\mathbf{Y}$ is implicit in the following:

$$\mathbf{Y} - b\mathbf{Y} - a - k = 0 \qquad\qquad [3.10]$$

As before I shall interpret [3.10] to represent a surface in 4-space:

$$\Phi(\mathbf{Y},a,b,k) = 0 \qquad\qquad [3.11]$$

Note that the degree of [3.10] (and hence [3.11]) is 2 and the number of terms in the algebraic representation of [3.11] is:

$$N = [(3 \times 4 \times 5 \times 6)/(1 \times 2 \times 3 \times 4)] - 1 = 14$$

Since [3.10] gives us four coefficients, the P-dimension of Model 1 with respect to Y is $14 - 4$ or 10. Here again the P-dimension with respect to C is the same as the P-dimension with respect to Y. It can be seen directly that Model 1 results from adding a single autonomous term to Model 3, thus Model 1 is a little more difficult to falsify.

Let us attempt to reduce the P-dimension of Model 3 even further by considering five cases. First, for Case 1, consider a 'material' reduction, i.e. specifying that the solution surfaces must pass through a particular pair of values for Y and C (without first specifying the values of b or k, since we do not know them). For example, we may know that this year's GNP is 100 and the level of consumption is 80, thus we can expect the surface to pass through $Y = 100$ and $C = 80$. Therefore, using [3.3a] and [3.4] yields:

$$0 = 100 - b100 - k$$
$$0 = 80 - b80 - bk$$

Hence at $Y = 100$ and $C = 80$ we have $b = 0.8$ and $k = 20$. I stress here that these values for b and k may only hold at $Y = 100$ and $C = 80$. So far we do not *know* anything about b and k – i.e. they are being considered *exogenous* variables. Now using equation [3.6] with these values of Y, b and k, yields:

$$A(100)^2 + B(0.8)^2 + D(20)^2 + E(16) + F(2000) + J(0.8) + M = 0 \quad [3.12]$$

Equation [3.12] can be used to eliminate one of the coefficients – i.e. solve for one coefficient in terms of the others. This means that there is now one less free coefficient, thus the P-dimension falls to five.

For Case 2, let us add to the model the common assumption that b remains the same for all observations although we still do not *know* its value. Constant parameters are almost always presumed in economic theories and my discussion already shows that such an extra assumption is not always necessary for testability. Since I am concerned exclusively with the *form* of models, in subsequent discussions remember that parameters (such as b) are never presumed to be fixed over all observations. However, for the purpose of discussing Case 2, we do assume b is fixed and thus the solution surface in terms of endogenous and exogenous variables becomes:

$$\Phi(\mathbf{Y}, k) = 0 \qquad\qquad [3.13]$$

that is, a 'surface' in 2-space. The general form is:

$$A\mathbf{Y} + Bk + D = 0 \qquad\qquad [3.14]$$

Since the solution [3.3] can be expressed as:

$$\mathbf{Y} - [1/(1-b)]k = 0 \qquad\qquad [3.3c]$$

we have values for two coefficients of equation [3.14] – the value for A and an expression of unknown value for B. This leaves D free to be chosen, thus we conclude that the P-dimension is now 1.

For Case 3, let us consider the additional assumption that $0 < b < 1$. This assumption can be combined with either Case 1 or Case 2. In each case the P-dimension will not change, however on the basis of Popper's subclass relation described in Chapter 2, we would say that this additional assumption makes the model 'more falsifiable' since it prohibits certain solutions. Nevertheless, it does not change the P-dimension!

Finally, for Case 4, let us consider an additional assumption that b is a particular value. For example, let us assume that $b = 0.5$. Thus equation [3.3c] becomes:

$$\mathbf{Y} - 0.5k = 0 \qquad\qquad [3.3d]$$

Therefore, we have values for both free coefficients of [3.14]. Hence the P-dimension is now zero and thus its testability is now maximum. This means that whenever this model is false, one observation is sufficient to refute the model. For example, the observation from Case 1 is not compatible with [3.3d] and hence if it was observed that $\mathbf{Y} = 100$ and $\mathbf{C} = 80$, the model would be falsified or refuted. By my formula, since $\delta = 1$, $\omega = 2$ and [3.3d] yields two terms (i.e. $t = 2$), the P-dimension can be determined as follows:

$$N = [(2 \times 3)/(1 \times 2)] - 1 = 2$$

hence the P-dimension equals $(2-2) = 0$.

Now let us turn to Model 2, which was also discussed in Chapter 2, but here I eliminate the identity [2.9]. As modified, Model 2 uses the following endogenous variables:

$\mathbf{Y} \equiv$ aggregate spending (i.e. GNP),
$\mathbf{C} \equiv$ aggregate consumption spending,
$\mathbf{K} \equiv$ aggregate spending on new capital.

Model 2

$$Y = C + K \tag{3.15}$$
$$C = a + bY \tag{3.16}$$
$$K = d/r \tag{3.17}$$

where a, b, d and r are considered exogenous variables.

The solutions for Y and C are implicit in the two following equations:

$$rY - brY - ra - d = 0 \tag{3.18}$$
$$rC - brC - bd - ar = 0 \tag{3.19}$$

Equation [3.18] represents the surface:

$$\Phi(Y, a, b, d, r) = 0 \tag{3.20}$$

and likewise, [3.19] represents:

$$\Phi(C, a, b, d, r) = 0 \tag{3.21}$$

These surfaces are in 5-space, their degree is 3, and for both there are four coefficients determined by equations [3.18] and [3.19] respectively. Thus the P-dimension can be calculated with respect to Y or C as follows:

$$N = [(4 \times 5 \times 6 \times 7 \times 8)/(1 \times 2 \times 3 \times 4 \times 5)] - 1 = 55$$

Hence the P-dimension is 55–4 = 51. However, the P-dimension with respect to K is not 51. Equation [3.17] itself is the solution for K and represents the surface:

$$\Phi(K, d, r) = 0 \tag{3.22}$$

Thus for K, the surface is in 3-space, and according to [3.17] the degree is 2. Two coefficients are thus determined and the P-dimension is calculated with respect to K as follows:

$$N = [(3 \times 4 \times 5)/(1 \times 2 \times 3)] - 1 = 9$$

hence the P-dimension is 9–2 = 7.

As I stated earlier, a theory (or model) as a whole is falsified when any statement deduced from it is falsified. Thus it can be concluded that the P-dimension of a model as a whole is the minimum P-dimension for each of its solution surfaces. Thus the P-dimension for Model 2 is 7, which is the P-dimension with respect to K.

It is interesting to note that not only is Model 2 considered 'better' than Model 1 by Popper's subclass relation, but also that the P-dimension is lower. Thus, judged by both criteria it can be concluded that Model 2 is 'better'.

2. Examples of the P-dimension in economic models

Let us form Model 4 by altering Model 2 somewhat by changing [3.17] to make the determination of **K** more interrelated as follows:

Model 4

$$Y = C + K \qquad [3.23]$$
$$C = a + bY \qquad [3.24]$$
$$K = d/r + eY \qquad [3.25]$$

which merely adds another exogenous parametric variable, e, to Model 2.

The solution for **Y** is implicit in the following:

$$rY - brY - erY - ar - d = 0 \qquad [3.26]$$

This represents a surface in 6-space of degree 3:

$$\Phi(Y,a,d,e,r) = 0 \qquad [3.27]$$

Equation [3.26] gives us 5 terms or coefficients, thus $N = 83$ and the P-dimension with respect to **Y** is 78.

The solution for **C** is implicit in:

$$rC - brC - erC - ar - aer - bd = 0 \qquad [3.28]$$

which represents:

$$\Phi(C,a,b,d,e,r) = 0 \qquad [3.29]$$

Since this is also in 6-space with degree 3 and [3.28] gives us 6 terms, the P-dimension with respect to **C** is 77. Likewise, the solution for **K** is implicit in:

$$rK - brK - erK - d + bd + aer = 0 \qquad [3.30]$$

which represents a surface of the same *form* as [3.29] thus the P-dimension with respect to **K** is also 77. I would conclude then that the P-dimension for the entire model is 77.

Next let us form Model 5 by altering Model 4 with a change in [3.24] as follows.

Model 5

$$Y = C + K \tag{3.31}$$
$$C = a + bY + fK \tag{3.32}$$
$$K = d/r + eY \tag{3.33}$$

which adds still another exogenous parametric variable, f.

The solution for **Y** is an equation with 7 terms whose highest degree is 4 and is in 7-space. Thus the P-dimension with respect to **Y** is 322. The solution for **C** is also in 7-space with degree 4 but has 12 terms, thus the P-dimension with respect to **C** is 317. And the solution for **K** yields 9 terms, thus the P-dimension with respect to **K** is 320. Thus I conclude that the P-dimension for Model 5 as a whole is 317.

Note how the interdependence of the relations of a model affects the P-dimension of the entire model. This leads to a consideration of one more alternative which is obtained by modifying Model 5 in a similar manner.

Model 6

$$Y = C + K \tag{3.34}$$
$$C = a + bY + fK \tag{3.35}$$
$$K = d/r + eY + gC \tag{3.36}$$

The implicit solution for **C** is a surface in 8-space:

$$\Phi(C,a,b,d,e,f,g,r) = 0 \tag{3.37}$$

The solution yields 10 terms and is of degree 4. Thus the P-dimension with respect to **C** is 484. Similarly, the solutions for **K** or **Y** yield the same P-dimension. Thus the P-dimension for Model 6 as a whole is 484.

Comparing Models 2, 4, 5 and 6 shows how the 'degree of interdependence' influences the P-dimension of a theory (or model). While the P-dimension of the rather simple Model 2 is 7, the P-dimension of the more complex Model 6 is 484. Consequently, there is a 65-fold increase in the number of observations necessary to form a sufficient falsification. To obtain some perspective on these numbers, let us consider how long it would take to make enough observations to construct a counter-example. If it takes one whole day to generate a new observation of all the variables in Model 6, then it would take over a year to construct a falsification!

Perhaps the six models considered so far are rather general if not outright dull. To spice things up a little, let us examine three of the many models developed by Jan Tinbergen [1956/67, appendix 3]. I have simplified them by eliminating the identities (which are definitions and hence contribute nothing of interest). These models will draw from the following list of variables:

$Y \equiv$ aggregate spending (i.e. GNP),
$P \equiv$ price level (index),
$W \equiv$ wage bill,
$N \equiv$ level of employment,
$C \equiv$ aggregate consumption spending,
$T \equiv$ total tax receipts.

Model 7 (closed, static, macro, money and product flow model)

$$Y = a\mathbf{P} + b\mathbf{Y} \qquad [3.38]$$
$$\mathbf{P} = \alpha + \beta(\mathbf{Y}/\mathbf{P}) \qquad [3.39]$$

where a, b, α and β are considered exogenous parametric variables [Tinbergen 1956/67, p. 231].

The unusual aspect of this model is that it involves fixed prices. The P-dimension with respect to $\mathbf{Y}$ is 49, and with respect to $\mathbf{P}$ it is 15. So this model's P-dimension is 15.

Model 8 (closed, static, macro, money, product and factor flow model)

$$\mathbf{Y} = a + b\mathbf{Y} + c\mathbf{W} \qquad [3.40]$$
$$\mathbf{W} = w\mathbf{N} \qquad [3.41]$$
$$\mathbf{N} = m + n\mathbf{Y} \qquad [3.42]$$

where a, b, c, m, n and w are considered exogenous parametric variables [p. 232].

For this model, the P-dimension with respect to $\mathbf{W}$ is 783, with respect to $\mathbf{Y}$ it is 324, and with respect to $\mathbf{N}$ it is 321.

Model 9 (closed, static, macro, money flow and public finance model)

$$\mathbf{Y} = \mathbf{C} + g \qquad [3.43]$$
$$\mathbf{C} = a + b(\mathbf{Y} - \mathbf{T}) \qquad [3.44]$$
$$\mathbf{T} = r + s\mathbf{Y} \qquad [3.45]$$

where a, b, g, r and s are considered exogenous parametric variables [p. 233].

For this model the P-dimension with respect to Y is 77, with respect to C it is 76, and with respect to T it is also 76.

There is not a lot that can be done to compare these three models since their respective fields of application vary widely. The P-dimension of Model 8, as well as Model 6, may seem large but as we shall see subsequently when we examine some more involved models these dimensions are not very high. It should be stressed that the P-dimension of a theory or model can be calculated only when all the relations are in an explicit form rather than an abstract form such as $C = f(Y)$. In fact, it could be argued that the P-dimension of a model involving abstract functions with no restrictions should be considered infinite (I will return to this consideration in Chapter 7).

Let us consider now a model which is usually presented with only abstract functions, but this time we will use explicit relations. (The model is a version of a Keynesian model originally presented by my thesis supervisor, Hans Brems [1959, pp. 34-47] but in which I have eliminated the one identity.) The endogenous variables for this model are as follows:

Y ≡ aggregate net spending,
C ≡ aggregate consumption spending,
I ≡ aggregate net investment spending,
L_T ≡ aggregate volume of 'transactions' cash balances,
L_L ≡ aggregate volume of 'assets' cash balances,
R ≡ the market interest rate.

Model 10

$$Y = C + I \qquad [3.46]$$
$$C = a + bY \qquad [3.47]$$
$$I^2 = c - eR^2 \qquad [3.48]$$
$$L_T = fY \qquad [3.49]$$
$$L_L = g/(R - h) \qquad [3.50]$$
$$m = L_T + L_L \qquad [3.51]$$

According to Brems [1959, p. 41], the solution of this model for Y is a fourth-degree equation *in* Y. The solution represents the following surface:

$$\Phi(\mathbf{Y},a,b,c,e,f,g,h,m) = 0 \qquad\qquad [3.52]$$

The leading term in his solution [p. 41] is $b^2 f^2 \mathbf{Y}4$, therefore the degree of the solution surface is 8. The solution has 27 terms and the surface is in 9-space. Thus the P-dimension with respect to $\mathbf{Y}$ is 24,282. I stress that this means that if the model is false, it will take 24,283 observations to refute it whenever we do not know the values of the parameters. Again, if it would take one entire day to generate a complete set of observations (i.e. one for each variable) then it would take over 66 years to construct a falsification. Stated another way, to be able to construct a falsification in one year would require the assembly of a complete set of observations every 21 minutes!

Note that the relations which contribute most to the high P-dimension are the equations [3.48] and [3.50]. Thus let us consider a couple of ways of altering them in order to reduce the P-dimension. First, let us change [3.48] to the following:

$$\mathbf{I} = c - e\mathbf{R} \qquad\qquad [3.48a]$$

This change causes the degree of equation [3.52] to fall to 4 and the number of terms to fall to 11. The P-dimension with respect to $\mathbf{Y}$ in turn falls to 703.

To go further, in addition to equation [3.48a], let us substitute a different relation for [3.50] (unfortunately this deviates considerably from the Keynesian 'liquidity preference' relation that Brems wished to model):

$$\mathbf{L}_L = g - h\mathbf{R} \qquad\qquad [3.50a]$$

With these two substitutions the P-dimension with respect to $\mathbf{Y}$ falls to 212.

Again, this shows how the *form* of the relations contribute to the P-dimension of a model. And again, while the P-dimension of Model 10 even before the modification seems rather high, I will subsequently show a model with an even higher dimension yet with fewer endogenous variables.

Consider a model which uses the well-known and popular Cobb-Douglas production function. We will see that one difficulty with models that use this function is that their P-dimensions become a function of the true (but unknown) value of one of their parameters.

Model 11

$$X = aN^{\lambda}k^{1-\lambda}, \quad 0 < \lambda < 1 \qquad [3.53]$$
$$N = b(W/p), \quad b > 0, p > 0 \qquad [3.54]$$
$$\partial X/\partial N = W/p \qquad\qquad [3.55]$$
$$Y = pX, \quad \text{(a definition)} \qquad [3.56]$$

where a, b, p and λ are parameters and thus the only endogenous variables are X (the level of real output), N (the level of employment), W (the money wage rate), and Y (the dollar value of the output).

The solution for Y is implicit in the following:

$$Y^{2-\lambda} - a^2 b^{\lambda} p^{2-\lambda} \lambda^{\lambda} k^{2-2\lambda} = 0 \qquad [3.57]$$

Now the 'degree' of this relation turns out to vary with λ. To facilitate the analysis let me assume that λ is a rational number, i.e. $\lambda = r/q$. Hence, the degree of [3.57] is $6q - r$. The P-dimension can thus be estimated as follows:

$$[(6q-r+1)(6q-r+2) \ldots (6q-r+6)/6!] - 3 \qquad [3.58]$$

since [3.57] is in 6-space and it has two terms.

The P-dimension with respect to Y can be calculated for several values of λ using expression [3.58] for each value.

Let us begin with an extreme case. If $\lambda = 0$ when $r = 0$ and $q = 1$, then the degree is 6. By expression [3.58] the P-dimension with respect to Y is:

$$[(7 \times 8 \times 9 \times 10 \times 11 \times 12)/(1 \times 2 \times 3 \times 4 \times 5 \times 6)] - 3 = 921$$

The other extreme case is $\lambda = 1$, and thus letting $r = 1$ and $q = 1$ yields a degree of 5. Therefore, in a similar manner, the calculated P-dimension is 459.

In the following five cases I will simply list the results. The cases are more reasonable values for λ if we are to maintain the form of [3.53].

if $\lambda = 1/2$, the degree is 11 and the P-dimension is 12,373,
if $\lambda = 2/3$, the degree is 16 and the P-dimension is 74,610,
if $\lambda = 1/3$, the degree is 17 and the P-dimension is 100,944,
if $\lambda = 3/4$, the degree is 21 and the P-dimension is 296,007,
if $\lambda = 1/4$, the degree is 23 and the P-dimension is 475,017.

Generally I note that the degree varies mostly with the denominator q. It may be concluded that the more complicated the rational number used to approximate λ, the less falsifiable is the solution. I also note that although when $\lambda = 3/4$ or $\lambda = 2/3$ is used to calculate **Y**, the results do not differ very much, however, the P-dimension does differ greatly.

I think I have shown enough examples to illustrate that some methodological decisions that model builders might make for the convenience of their mathematical analysis can lead to extremely unfortunate methodological consequences whenever one also is concerned with the requirement of testability. Of course, it will be noted that my discussion has been concerned only with explicit non-stochastic equilibrium models and thus may have a limited applicability. I would agree that my discussion and my concept of a P-dimension is seen in the clearest light in terms of these types of models, but it can be noted also that stochastic econometric models are typically constructed from similar non-stochastic equilibrium models. The degree of testability of any econometric model is not independent of the P-dimension of its underlying exact model. Such an interdependence, I claim, is implicit in the econometrician's consideration of the so-called 'Identification Problem'.

3. The identification problem and the P-dimension

Econometricians have long recognized that the problem of identification is logically prior to the problem of estimation of the parameters of a model [e.g. Johnston 1963, Goldberger 1964, Fisher 1966]. One of the purposes of this chapter is to support the claim that the methodological problem concerning truth status, which is connected with our discussion of the P-dimension, is logically prior to the problem of identification. There might appear to be an obvious objection to the relevance of this claim – namely that the econometrician is concerned with stochastic models and I have been dealing with only non-stochastic models so far. It can, however, be pointed out that the problem of identification exists quite apart from the stochastic nature of econometric models [Johnston 1963, p. 243].

In order to support adequately my claim, I will first outline the problem of identification since today it is too often taken for granted. To discuss this problem, I have at my disposal the well-developed language of the econometrician. So far I have chosen to avoid using such terminology so as to avoid suggesting an econometric methodology. Here may be a good place to start, so I note that the methodology of econometric model building is concerned with the following concepts: a structure, a model, and a property called 'identification'. By a structure (of a non-stochastic model) I mean 'a specific set of structural equations' such as is obtained by giving specific numerical values to the parameters of a model. By a (non-stochastic) model I mean 'only a specification of the form of the structural equations (for instance, their linearity and a designation of the variables occurring in each equation).... More abstractly, a model can be defined as a set of structures' [Koopmans 1953, p. 29]. Identification refers to the property of a specific model which assures that, if the model is posited as being the hypothetical 'generator' of the observed data, a *unique* structure can be deduced (or identified) from the observed data. By hypothetical generator I mean that if one is given the true values of the parameters then whenever the observed values of the exogenous variables are put into the model, the resulting values for the endogenous variables are said to be 'generated' by the structure of the model.

There are two ways in which a model may fail to possess the identification property. Either the model is such that no structure can be deduced, or the model is such that more than one structure can be deduced from the same data. Attempting to avoid the possibility of these difficulties is called the 'problem of identification'.

First I wish to pursue the significance of the claim made by many econometricians that the problem of identification is logically prior to the estimation problem; that it would exist even if our samples were infinitely large; and that it would exist even with non-stochastic models. The task of the econometrician is to determine the particular structure of a specified model (usually a linear model) which would generate the given data. A possible methodological problem, usually called the 'problem of estimation', is that the data given is stochastic and hence the structure cannot be exactly determined. But before the structure (i.e. the parameters) of a model can be estimated, the form of the model must have been specified such that the problem of identification is avoided. Thus we can see that the problem of identification is 'logically prior to the estimation problem'. I note further here that the consideration of the property of identification implies (or is predicated on the assumption) that the model in question is known (or assumed) to be true. Hence the solution statements are true statements, and although there exists a finite P-dimension, no set of observations could ever be found which would contradict the model.

It is this 'assumed truth status' of the form which is the moot point of this section. This is the epistemological problem concerning truth status that I mentioned at the beginning of Chapter 2. Since the form of the model must be assumed to be true before the problem of identification is considered, it can be concluded that the epistemological problem concerning truth status (the truth status of the form of a model) is logically prior to the problem of identification.

Note that the solution to the identification problem amounts to the avoidance of 'generally' (in an algebraic sense) in a solution statement of a model. A solution is general when it remains invariant under transformations of the coordinates (i.e. of the model). Thus the uniqueness property of identification implies a lack of invariance.

Identifiability is dependent upon the form of the model. As most texts on econometrics indicate, what can determine the identifiability of a model is the relationship between the number of endogenous variables and the number of exogenous variables. Avoidance of the identification problem requires that the relationship be of a nature which will assure us that with a finite number of observations we can (if the model is true) deduce the values of the parameters (i.e. the structure). This requirement holds even for non-stochastic models. If for a particular model this requirement were not met then it may be possible that even if both the number of observations were infinite (or unlimited) and the model were true, we still could not deduce the unique structure of the model (i.e. distinguish between the possible sets of parameter values). The finite number of observations that are necessary to deduce a structure of a non-stochastic model is analogous to the concept which I have called the P-dimension.

Although in this chapter the discussion has been limited to non-stochastic models (hence avoiding the problem of estimation) it was not limited to only directly or indirectly linear models (as would most econometric methodology). The discussion applies to all linear and non-linear models or relations between the endogenous and exogenous variables, although the specific formula for calculating the P-dimension has only been worked out for polynomial solutions.

One of the implications of the priority of the methodological problem concerning truth status over the identification problem is that econometric studies are not substitutes for research in pure theory. Clearly, econometrics is very useful for practical applications of economic theories, particularly in the area of economic planning and forecasting. Many economists unfortunately confuse the sophistication of the statistical theory of econometrics with the sophistication of the economic theory upon which the econometric model is based. The fact is that the economic theory used in econometric studies is usually very primitive. If progress is to be made in pure theory, it will be more through our efforts to deal with the methodological problem concerning truth status than the problems of econometrics.

4. Concluding remarks about the P-dimension

The most important statement to be deduced from a model is the solution. The solution, or its form, specifies that the endogenous variables are related to the parameters and exogenous variables in a specific manner. Models which differ will specify different relations – i.e. different solutions. Methodologically speaking, theories can be compared by comparing the form of the solution statements deduced from their representative models. I have suggested that the operative comparative question is: What is required to show that the *form* of a model (indicated by the solution) is false?

If the solution statement is false, then in principle (or conceivably) we can show the solution to be false. Using the P-dimension criterion one can state exactly what it takes to refute the solution statement (i.e. the minimum but sufficient number of observations). If the solution statement is true, a similar quantitative criterion *cannot* be established to specify the finite number of observations which would be sufficient to *assure* that whenever the values of the parameters are unknown, the solution statement is indeed true. One cannot distinguish between false or true solution statements on the basis of their form if the number of observations is less than the P-dimension.

From the illustrations presented earlier in this chapter, it is easy to see that the two factors which most influence the P-dimension are the degree of, and the number of variables or parameters in, the solution equation. The degree is influenced by the form of every relation in the model and the 'degree of interdependence' of the relations in the model. The 'degree of interdependence' also influences the number of parameters since as variables were added to a relation we usually added extra parameters (see the discussion of Models 2, 4, 5 and 6 on pp. 72-4). I suggest that what is usually called 'simplicity' might be interpreted in terms of my illustrations [see also Popper 1959/61, Ch. 7]. Certainly, reducing the degree of interdependence makes the model 'more simple'. Likewise, the paucity of parameters is usually an indication of simplicity. I say 'usually' because, as Model 11 (p. 78) illustrates, this is not necessarily the case.

In this sense the desire for simplicity can be translated into a desire for higher degrees of testability or falsifiability. I would like to be able to make such a translation of the concept of algebraic or mathematical simplicity of the forms of the relations of a model but as can be seen with Model 11, although the 'form' does not change with changing values of the exponents of equation [3.53] the P-dimension (and hence falsifiability) can change. Therefore one cannot always be sure that the form alone indicates anything. However, the desire for pragmatic simplicity (i.e. the ease with which one can solve for the endogenous variables) can be translated into the desire for lower P-dimensions. As was seen in the case of Model 10 (p. 76), by reducing the degree of the solution equation, the equation is made easier to solve and at the same time more falsifiable.

It might be argued that the proposed criteria (i.e. Popper's subclass relation and my P-dimension) is useful only to compare *comparable* models rather than evaluate a single model. One answer to this objection is that although I did not (and probably cannot) develop an absolute criterion using the P-dimension concept, one does get the strong impression that a model with a P-dimension in the order of 100,000, or even 10,000, is approaching what some economists might call a 'tautological' model since it would be very difficult to refute such a model convincingly. Of course, if economists adopt the aim of science that is posited by the Popper-Socrates view, then the concepts of falsifiability and P-dimension are crucial. If, on the other hand, economists maintain that the aim of science is to provide verifiable theories and models [e.g. Machlup 1955, Rotwein 1959] then the necessity to investigate the P-dimension of their economic models and theories is less obvious. However, I noted at the beginning of Chapter 2 that verificationists may not wish to waste time on tautologies so it might be suggested that the P-dimension is important for the verificationists as well. Although a model with a P-dimension of 100,000 is in principle falsifiable, in some crude sense it is 'more tautological' than a model with a P-dimension of only 10.

In terms of the Popper-Socrates view of science, one can hardly *know* when one has made a mistake (i.e. when one has put forth a false theory) if it takes over 100,000 observations in order to show that the theory is false. This observation is even more significant when it is recognized that all of these models are non-stochastic and thus in principle refutable with a finite set of observations. Further consideration of the methodological problems introduced by stochasticism is postponed until Chapters 7 and 8.

Based on the discussion in Chapters 1 and 2 and on the illustrations of the present chapter, it might still be argued that the truth status of some non-stochastic models can in principle be determined. But unfortunately, it is only the falsity that can be demonstrated. However, the Popper-Socrates philosophy of science would have us being very pleased that at least some models are falsifiable and that we can potentially make progress in science by learning from our 'mistakes' – that is, from the refutations of our models and theories. Despite the lofty platitudes embodied in this optimistic philosophy, many economists may still see the worship of falsifiability as a misplaced desire for the hole instead of the donut!

In Chapters 4 and 5, I deal with how economists maintain a more positive interest in the truth status of models. While it is widely recognized that it is usually impossible to prove that a model or theory is true – even a non-stochastic model – economists still wish their theories to achieve some sort of truth status. In Chapter 4, I examine how theorists accommodate questions of the truth status of theories by employing more conventional standards than those embodied in the Popper-Socrates view of science. Of particular concern will be the nature of methodological disputes in the absence of a means of demonstrating the truth status of competing models or theories. In Chapter 5, I explain how an economist might view questions of theory choice when truth status cannot be directly demonstrated. Of particular concern will be the failure of conventional substitutes to overcome the problem of demonstrating the truth status of models (or theories) when they are true.

PART II

Popper-Samuelson Demarcation vs the Truth Status of Models

4

Conventionalism and Economic Theory: Methodological Controversy in the 1960s

> If perfect competition is the best simple theory in town, that is no excuse for saying we should regard it as a good theory if it is not a good theory.... We must not impose a regularity – or approximate regularity – in the complex facts which is not there. Good science discerns regularities and simplicities that are there in reality ... psychological usefulness should not be confused with empirical validity.
>
> Paul A. Samuelson [1963, p. 236]

> It would be highly desirable to have a more general theory than Marshall's.... The theory of imperfect or monopolistic competition developed by Chamberlin and Robinson is an attempt to construct such a more general theory. Unfortunately, it possesses none of the attributes that would make it a truly useful general theory.
>
> Milton Friedman [1953, p. 38]

While theorists and applied economists may dutifully assure themselves that their models are indeed falsifiable, the truth status of their models continues to present an ongoing methodological problem. The model builder must make decisions regarding three things: (1) the question to be answered by his or her model, (2) the list of variables and the specification which are endogenous and which are exogenous, and (3) how the truth status of the answers will be determined.

Within any model or theory an individual idea is usually represented by a verbal, or mathematical, statement. A statement is true only if it corresponds to facts, that is, only if there will never be a fact which contradicts it. Of course, for a model or theory to be true it is necessary, but not sufficient, that it be internally consistent. There is a popular school of thought in the philosophy of science which would equate truth status with internal consistency, since it would appear that truth status is only a matter of convention [see Agassi 1963, 1966a; Boland 1982, Ch. 1]. This view of science – often called 'conventionalism' – is a rather sophisticated version of an old theory of knowledge. The old theory – sometimes called 'empiricism' and other times 'inductivism' – said that knowledge is (or represents) the accumulation of empirical facts and as such is necessarily true. The newer conventionalism says that all knowledge is accumulated facts but true theoretical knowledge is impossible. Conventionalism says that truth status is at best a matter of convention because we can never know that a theory is true.

It is important to distinguish conventionalism from an equally popular doctrine that sounds similar – specifically, Milton Friedman's 'instrumentalism' [Friedman 1953, see also Boland 1979a]. Fortunately, it is easy to distinguish these two methodological doctrines. Conventionalism is concerned with the *status* of theories and models and instrumentalism is concerned with the *role* of theories and models. Where conventionalism asserts that theories are neither true nor false but only better or worse, instrumentalism asserts that if the theory or model works its truth status does not matter. According to instrumentalism, theories and models should be judged on the basis of whether or not they are useful. This distinction gets rather blurred in practice, since it is possible for someone to embrace both views. One can advocate conventionalism when asked about the truth status of a model and advocate instrumentalism when asked about the role of models in economic science. It is possible to advocate instrumentalism and reject conventionalism. However, most economists seem to embrace both. When they say Theory A is 'better' than Theory B, it is not always clear whether they mean Theory A is better as measured on some scale of truth-likeness or as measured on some scale of usefulness. When advocates of conventionalism argue methodology with followers of Friedman's instrumentalism, it is not always clear what the argument is about.

When I began publishing articles in economics journals in the 1960s, the number of methodologists in our profession was very small. Among this small group there was one remaining apriorist, the late Ludwig von Mises, and a few empiricists struggling against apriorism. Everyone else battled empiricism by endorsing some form of conventionalism and/or Friedman's instrumentalism. In 1970 I reported that the battle was over. Conventionalism and instrumentalism had won out over empiricism. The last remaining General for the empiricists, Eugene Rotwein, was by then pleading for toleration and 'pluralism' [Rotwein 1966]. Although the number of methodologists is now much larger and growing, things have not changed very much. Most methodological disputes still disgorge very little substance. What the victory over empiricism means for economic theory and the prospects for a continued occupation in the face of rising interest in the Popper-Socrates view of science will be the topic of this chapter.

The major outcome of the victory of conventionalism and instrumentalism over empiricism in the late 1960s was that methodological controversy in economics was reduced to nit-picking over which must come first – simplicity or generality. The popular 1960s controversy was a pseudo-argument. Both sides argued from the same methodological position, namely, conventionalism.

1. Robinsonian conventionalism

Except for a small group of economists whose credentials are probably suspect anyway, all economists can still be divided into two groups: those who say they agree with Milton Friedman's famous methodology essay [1953] and those who do not. Closer examination shows, however, that both groups espouse the conventionalist view which sees science as a series of approximations to a demonstrated accord with reality. Their dispute in fact is simply a conventionalist family disagreement over conventionalist criteria for judging theories. Namely, it is a dispute between the conservative followers of Friedman who advocate simplicity as the more important criterion for judging theories, and the would-be liberal conventionalists who argue in favour of generality as the more important criterion. The generalists are perhaps inspired by Paul Samuelson's views [1952, 1963, 1965] of economic methodology and his apparent success at demonstrating the logical validity of a proposition by generalizing it.

Being a beginner in the 1960s, I did not understand *why* simplicity or generality was considered desirable. Later I was to learn that the dispute was, more specifically, a dispute between those who wished to promote mathematical interest in economics vs those concerned with promoting the application of economics to real-world problems and phenomena [see also Grubel and Boland 1986]. Real-world applications of economics are almost always facilitated by simplifications. Those guided by the aesthetic tastes of mathematics departments were more interested in the generalization of economic theories. For example, rather than explaining the choice between two specific goods (apples vs bananas), we should explain the choice between *n* different goods. Unfortunately, I was misled by the political environment of the 1960s. I assumed that the conservative-liberal schism was a reflection of politics and ideology and thus would be expressed in terms of theoretical disputes between the so-called 'Chicago School' and more liberal views of theory such as those found in Cambridge (England or Massachusetts).

The dispute over methodology in the 1960s appeared to me to have its genesis in Edward Chamberlin's and Joan Robinson's attempts to modify the old Marshallian theory of the firm [Chamberlin 1933, Robinson 1933]. The question for the 'Robinsonian conventionalist', as I shall call the disputants, is the following: Should we (1) stick to the Marshallian 'perfect competition' model of the firm (or perhaps a 'pure monopoly' model or a 'mixture of the two' [Friedman 1953, p. 36] – whichever 'works'), or (2) adopt the more modern 'imperfect competition' model of the firm?

Perfect competition, of course, is characterized by very small independent firms in a very large open (i.e. free enterprise) market such that any one firm cannot affect the price for the good it produces. By contrast, imperfect competition is characterized by the ability of any firm to affect its price by varying the amount of its good it supplies in the market. One model is more simple, the other is more general.

I have called the parties of this dispute Robinsonian conventionalists because it was Joan Robinson's attempted modification which makes the dispute more clear-cut. Her efforts made it possible for us to understand better the old perfect competition theory of the firm.

2. Pareto optimality

Now, it is a well-known principle of welfare economics that if all markets were cases of perfect competition and all firms were to maximize their profit as well as everyone maximizing their personal satisfaction, then in the long run we would have achieved an economic optimum, often called a 'Pareto optimum' – namely, an optimum where no one can gain by any redistribution of resources between firms without someone else losing. Sometimes this is called a *'laissez-faire* optimum' because here everyone is given leave to independently pursue his or her own business whether it be profit or self-satisfaction.

The theory of the firm in this case is very simple. We ask: Why is the firm producing at its present level of output? We answer: Because, given the going prices in the market and its technical capabilities, that is the one level of output which maximizes its profit. And the truth status of this answer is determined merely by assuming perfect competition and that costs facing the firm are guided by diminishing marginal returns to all factors of production. That is all there is to that!

The appeal of this simple theory to the conservative economist should be obvious. It says, if we can satisfy the marginal conditions of maximization with perfect competition, the best of all possible worlds will be achieved both in terms of ends and of means. In terms of ends we have the Pareto welfare optimum (no one can gain without others losing) and in terms of means we have complete independence (i.e. classical Liberalism).

The case of imperfect competition, which everyone agrees is 'more realistic', is, however, much more complicated. It is more complicated merely because we cannot say 'given the going prices in the market' since the firm's decision affects its prices as well as its level of output. And so the prices are not 'given'. Instead, the answer would be: Given the behaviour of the prices in the market as well as the firm's technical capabilities, the firm produces the one level of output which maximizes its profit. Clearly, this is not much of a change in the theory, but to determine the truth status of this modified theory of the firm we must add assumptions about the behaviour of prices and the firm's ability to affect its prices, as well as assumptions about its technical cost constraints. There are many ways to do this, thus any way we choose is likely to be *ad hoc*. Moreover, the *ad hoc* conditions usually place more demands on our concept of the market than most economists admit [see Arrow 1959, Clower 1959, Richardson 1959, Boland 1986]. And to satisfy these demands we must make behavioural assumptions about factors outside the firm which increases both the complexities and the difficulties in deducing testable predictions. In mathematical terms, we can see that the complexities are created by allowing for the variability of prices. That is, we now have one more dependent variable, in addition to output level, which affects the decision criterion, i.e. profit. In terms of an old jargon, there has been an increase in the degrees of freedom.

3. Welfare implications of imperfect competition

Now what about the welfare implications of the modified theory? These turn out to be another problem. The modified theory does not necessarily lead in the long run to a Pareto optimum. Furthermore, it allows for interdependence between firms and customers. However, virtually everyone agrees that such non-optimality and such complexity is the nature of the 'real world'. For all its potential drawbacks, this theory of imperfect competition has, as a limiting case, the other theory – namely, the perfectly competitive theory of the firm. Thus imperfect competition is claimed to be 'more general'. The price of generality is the reduction of simplicity – there are additional variables and *ad hoc* assumptions to deal with.

4. The conventionalist controversy

I think I can now clinch my point that the 1960s methodological controversy did not amount to much. On the one side we have the pro-perfect competition theorists, the methodological conservatives who believe in simplicity, and on the other side we have the would-be methodological liberals who believe in generality. Surely the conservatives could never convince the pro-imperfect competition theorists of the virtue of simplicity by merely asserting that simplicity is more virtuous than generality. Such, however, would seem to be the case. When Friedman, in his famous 1953 essay on methodology, argues that greater generality of a set of assumptions does not matter if the alternative set of simple assumptions leads to positive results and predictions, he is merely reaffirming his methodological position [see Boland 1979a]. Moreover, he tells us that assumptions, and hence the results, are only approximations anyway, and thus we should stick to our perfect competition models of the firm because they are capable of providing more positive results [Friedman 1953, p. 38]. Followers of Friedman go on to argue that with the complex imperfect competition theory and its degrees of freedom and *ad hoc* conditions, it is difficult to come up with any results or predictions, positive or otherwise [see Stigler 1963, Archibald 1961].

After all this, what can be argued by the Robinsonian conventionalists who advocate generality and its embodiment in the idea of imperfect competition? While Samuelson says that the task of an economic theory of the firm is 'describing and summarizing empirical reality' [Samuelson 1952, 1967] he nevertheless argues that all 'scientists accept some degree of approximation' [Samuelson 1964] and thus he admits that all theories are approximations. And some followers of Friedman continue to say that imperfect competition is empty or arbitrary, and since it is only an approximation, we should be guided only by simplicity [e.g. Stigler 1963] and thereby see that the perfectly competitive theory is to be preferred.

Since both schools are thus immersed in the same kind of difficulty when they attempt to criticize either theory, the issue becomes which is a 'better approximation' – a simplifying approximation which gives more positive results, or a generalizing approximation which allows for a better description of what firms (in fact) do? From the standpoint of the Robinsonian conventionalists, it is not sufficient merely to assert that simplicity is more important than generality or vice versa – and so the conventionalist controversy must continue.

5. Limitations of approximating *laissez-faire*

I do not propose to resolve this methodological dispute here, mainly because I think the simple perfect competition theory of the firm is simply false and the imperfect competition theory is at best pointless. The perfect competition theory is false, if for no other reason, because above all it assumes that all firms are so small relative to the market that they individually cannot affect their prices. The imperfect competition theory is pointless because it is far from complete and unlikely to be completed as a 'partial equilibrium' theory of the firm [see Boland 1986]. So, I will turn to the broader methodological question of approximation underlying both positions in the controversy. In this regard I will try to draw an analogy between this question of approximation and the 1960s theory of approximate free trade (which was called the theory of the Second Best [see Meade 1955, Lipsey and Lancaster 1956-7, Mishan 1960 and the bibliography in Bohm 1967] and is about the possible outcomes of approximating the goals of any economic system).

Let me explain the theory of the Second Best in terms appropriate for the construction of my analogy. The 'first best' is the *laissez-faire* optimum where everyone is individually optimizing (i.e. maximizing utility or profit) and hence society as a whole is at an optimum. If the 'first best' cannot be reached because there is a constraining obstacle to satisfying all the optimizing conditions that are necessary for the achievement of a Pareto optimum (e.g. a constraint preventing the firm from setting its marginal cost to exactly equal its marginal revenue), then Second Best Theory says that (1) between the resulting 'constrained' outcome reached by approximating the completion of the optimizing conditions and the 'first best' outcome, there exists a 'second best' outcome, but (2) in order to reach the 'second best' outcome we must give up the method followed to reach the 'first best'.

For example, if for any reason some of the firms in the economy cannot satisfy all its marginal conditions for maximization because of some legal constraints (such as union constraints and/or price controls), the economy as a whole will not be at a Pareto optimum. That is, there would be the possibility that without the legal constraints someone could gain without anyone else losing. Now, if we require that all other firms (those not restricted by the legal constraints) must still satisfy the marginal conditions of (profit) maximization, then (it is argued) there will necessarily be the possibility of choosing some other set of possible decisions on the part of the non-restricted firms which will leave the economy as a whole better off than would be the case if they attempted to satisfy all the conditions for individual maximization of profit. The asserted existence of the possibility of improving over the approximation of economic optimum is the central idea of the 'theory of the Second Best' which asserts that approximation in this case is less than 'second best'. The argument supporting this theory, which unfortunately is somewhat mathematically involved, can be found in Lipsey and Lancaster [1956-7].

On the basis of the implications of this theory it turns out that one of the virtues of the perfect competition optimum was that it involved a unique method for reaching the optimum. That is, there is one and only one allocation of resources, and one and only one distribution of commodities between consumers and between producers. Giving up the perfect competition model (and its optimum) involves giving up the uniqueness of the choice regarding methods (criteria, conditions, etc.) for allocation and distribution. For this reason, McManus [1959] states a conventionalist argument that the approximated optimum is a desirable 'third best' because at least we know how to reach it while we only know of the possibility of the 'second best'.

The theory of the existence and method of the 'second best' arose in the 1950s when someone was considering traditional free trade arguments [see Meade 1955]. The issue then was the following dilemma: We all agree that if every country pursued a free trade policy (e.g. no tariffs or quotas) then we would have the best of all possible economic worlds. The question arose, if one country can gain by instituting tariffs (such as an import duty on all foreign-produced goods), what should other countries do? The free trade people maintained that the best we can do is approximate free trade. That is, every other country should not respond by also instituting tariffs, but should behave as if every country did not have tariffs. Now this argument is merely one of many possible theories, and Second Best Theory was offered as a counter-theory that there does exist a better way of trading although it will not be the 'first best' way.

6. Second best theory vs approximationism

At first it seemed curious to me that I could not find much in the writings of the Robinsonian conventionalists such as Friedman or Samuelson about the theory of the Second Best – particularly since the issue is approximation. I think the reason for this lacuna is that Robinsonian conventionalism and Second Best Theory are not compatible. To see this we have to raise the theory of the Second Best to a meta-theoretical level. Robinsonian conventionalism of either school (liberal or conservative) says that approximating an ideal or optimum (such as simplicity or generality) is the best we can do, and therefore is satisfactory. My meta-theoretical formulation of the well-known Second Best Theory is: There does exist something better than the approximation of the 'ideal' theory (i.e. of the exact representation of empirical reality) but to find it we are required to give up the old method (namely, Robinsonian conventionalism).

What are the implications of this meta-theory for the dispute over the theory of the firm? I have already noted that there are obstacles to the construction of competitive theories of the firm (one is false, the other is arbitrary) thus my second best meta-theory says that there must exist a better theory than the two discussed, but it must be something other than a mixture of the two or a modification of one of them.

7. The simplicity-generality trade-off

What will be the Robinsonian conventionalists' argument against my meta-theoretical formulation? It may be something of the form: Yes, there may be a better way, but the current version of conventionalism is the best we can do! And we begin an infinite regress. Or they may argue (as some followers of Friedman do) that the 'first best' has not been reached because there are obstacles to perfect competition and so, they say, get rid of the obstacles. In other words, they might argue that people and firms, in short the whole world, should behave in accordance with the 'ideal' theory in order that the theory will be true.

It is more likely that the methodological conservatives will argue that my meta-theoretical formulation is simply wrong because (1) Second Best Theory is about welfare with commodities and my second best meta-theory is about knowledge with theories, and (2) the perfect vs imperfect competition dispute does not have its analogue at the meta-theoretical level. In response to such an argument I would have to say that it is much easier for conventionalists to see an analogy between welfare and knowledge and between commodities and theories than it would for other methodologists. This is because the conventionalists' approach to meta-theoretical questions resembles the economists' approach to welfare questions (as I will explain in Chapter 5).

It is clearly a conventionalist characterization that the methodological problem of choosing between theories involves some sort of 'trade-off' between generality and simplicity. Such a statement of the methodological problem as an economic problem is precisely what Martin Bronfenbrenner argued when he told us that to improve a theory by one criterion (e.g. simplicity) we must give up some of the other criterion (e.g. generality, which he sees as a hallmark of an opposing 'realistic' school) at an increasing rate [Bronfenbrenner 1966]. It is as if we are constrained along a methodological possibilities frontier analogous to a standard economic concept of the production possibilities frontier. Furthermore, Bronfenbrenner tells us that the choice reduces to a matter of 'subjective preference', that is, subjective optimization. In other words, the conventionalists themselves have raised the economic argument to the meta-theoretical level.

As far as the second possible major objection goes, I simply note that at the meta-theoretical level the conventionalists reduce the original dispute to an argument concerning criteria for judging theories. To pick the perfect competition theory is to optimize simplicity, and to pick the imperfect competition theory is to optimize generality. Here there is no compromise. Given that the choice of theories leads to combinations of levels of simplicity and generality which are constrained along an efficiency frontier, as Bronfenbrenner suggests, the 'ideal' theory, i.e. the methodological optimum (if it exists), is somehow an intermediate between the two extremes, a 'half-way house' as he calls it. I would like to extend this analysis further. The choice of the 'ideal' theory for a compromising Robinsonian conventionalist such as Bronfenbrenner implies the satisfaction of some Pareto-like conditions. Such a condition in this case would be the equality between the relative subjective preference for simplicity vs generality and the marginal rate of methodological substitution of generality for simplicity within the constraint of the methodological possibilities frontier. To reach the half-way house 'ideal' within the Robinsonian conventionalist dispute requires the 'ideal' theory to be a mixture of the two extreme theories (such as allowing imperfection in the factor market but assuming perfect competition in the product market, or the other way around, etc.). I think this optimization methodology is wrong-headed. The solution to this dispute is to get rid of the meta-theoretical constraint in order to be able to increase *both* simplicity and generality. The meta-theoretical constraint results from attempting to resolve the dispute within Robinsonian conventionalism. My suggestion is, of course, what my second best meta-theory suggests. It is also what I think Popper suggests in that it is what underlies his saying that simplicity and generality go together (see Chapter 2).

8. Concluding remarks on Robinsonian conventionalism

To conclude, the primary methodological dispute of the 1960s, which I have called the Robinsonian conventionalist dispute, forced the argument over theories of the firm to be concerned with conventionalist criteria for judging theories. Furthermore, the dispute constrained the choice of theories within the Robinsonian dispute (i.e. perfect vs imperfect competition). Optimization within this meta-theoretical constraint would lead to a mixture of the two theories but there exist obstacles to the success of such a mixture – the ingredients are one false theory and one *ad hoc* and unnecessarily arbitrary theory. By means of the theory of the Second Best I have suggested that the pursuit of a theory of the firm within the constraint of the Robinsonian conventionalist methodology leads to a 'third best' – a mixture of the two disputed theories. And that there exists a 'second best' which can only be achieved by stepping outside (Robinsonian) conventionalist methodology.

5

Methodology as an Exercise in Economic Analysis

the problem which I tried to solve by proposing the criterion of falsifiability was neither a problem of meaningfulness or significance, nor a problem of truth or acceptability. It was the problem of drawing a line ... between the statements, or systems of statements, of the empirical sciences, and all other statements.

Karl R. Popper [1965, p. 39]

Methodology has always occupied a precarious position in academic circles. It is neither only a study of applied logic nor is it only a sociological matter. For me, methodology is the study of the relationships between problems and solutions and between questions and answers. Clearly, logic plays an important role in any methodology, but logic alone would not be sufficient for a complete study. There are many methodological decisions to be made which are neither arbitrary nor irrational. Such decisions occupy a central place in the domain of any methodological study. Of particular interest, it seems to me, is the distinction between intended and unintended consequences of a decision to use a particular method to solve a particular problem or to answer a particular question.

This view of methodology is intended to avoid all the linguistic philosophy that usually goes under the name of methodology. I want to avoid this primarily because I find it unilluminating and uninteresting. I would also like to avoid all the authoritarian appeals to 'rules to promote scientific progress' which individuals, whom we might call 'pseudo-Popperians', might claim to offer with their demands for 'refutability'.

In this chapter, I attempt to illustrate a different view of the Popper-Socrates philosophy of science by presenting a methodological critique of the conventionalist methodology discussed in Chapter 4. I continue to study conventionalist methodology because, though it is quite uninteresting, it remains popular. While conventionalist methodology may, for the reason of popularity, be applied to economics, I think it is uninteresting precisely because it attempts to solve such uninteresting philosophical problems as choosing the 'best' theory from a set of competing theories where 'best' is interpreted as a status representing the highest attainable point on a truth-likeness scale. I want to show that the conventionalist methodological problem, if specified completely, will be found to be unsolvable on its own terms. Again, my argument will be that the conventionalist methodological problem is, methodologically speaking, the same problem that welfare economics theory attempts to solve. The welfare problem is to choose the optimum among competing alternatives. In economics it would be to choose the optimum (possible) state of the economy by means of criteria applied to the allocation of resources. In conventionalist methodology it is to choose the optimum (conceivable) theory by means of criteria applied to the selection of hypotheses or models.

1. Conventionalist methodology

Now let me briefly describe and explain the practice of conventionalist methodology among economists in terms more general than the discussion in Chapter 4. As I noted at the beginning of Chapter 4, economists when confronted by practical problems of applied economics will follow the methodological doctrine of instrumentalism [see Boland 1979a]. In effect, instrumentalism asserts primarily that theories merely play a role as tools or instruments used to solve practical problems or as learning (i.e. heuristic) devices so as to get at the facts more efficiently, and so on. With tools or heuristic devices the question of truth status is considered of less importance than questions about usefulness. Economists when confronting the philosophical problems of economic theory will follow the doctrine of conventionalism [see Boland 1979a, 1982]. Conventionalism asserts primarily that theories are merely catalogues or files of facts. That is, theories are neither (absolutely) true nor false. When viewing theories, both doctrines will pose the methodological problem of choosing the 'better' of any two available theories. Each doctrine seeks a set of criteria or principles to use as a guide for making the (optimum) choice but the choice criteria may be very different.

In economics there are two different approaches to the problem of choice, both of which may be applied to both doctrines. When I was a student in the 1960s, one approach was called the Theory of Choice and was attributed to Walras, Pareto, Hicks and maybe even Marshall. The other was called the Theory of Revealed Preference and was widely attributed to Samuelson [1938, 1948] (see also Georgescu-Roegen [1954]). In the Theory of Choice one would attempt to explain why a particular choice logically follows from a specified set of principles regarding the behaviour of the person(s) making the choice. In the Theory of Revealed Preference one would attempt to infer from the fact that a person has made a particular choice what his or her reasons must have been for that choice. (Actually, the latter approach can only infer the specifications of the principles assumed in a Theory of Choice [see Samuelson 1950b].)

In methodology the analogue of this distinction between approaches is found in the difference between some popular versions of Popper's philosophy of science [e.g. Blaug 1968, 1980; Tarascio and Caldwell 1979; Caldwell 1982] and Thomas Kuhn's philosophy of science [1962/70]. The popular (mis)readings of Popper to which I refer are analogous to a Theory of Choice. It is alleged that certain choices follow from the Popper-Socrates theory of learning and Popper's view of the logic of theories (see also Chapter 2). Kuhn's view is that a particular choice is revealed as preferred by the contents of the standard textbooks of any discipline [Agassi 1971b]. Of course, followers of Kuhn would attempt to infer the significance of the choice of a textbook based on the methodological principles of conventionalism which I noted above. Ultimately, however, the two approaches boil down to the same thing – a set of specified principles for making a choice.

2. Choice in welfare economics

Like my argument in Chapter 4, I wish to draw an analogy between ideas in economic theories of social choice and a basic idea of conventionalist methodology of theory choice. To set up the analogy, I will discuss the economist's theoretical view of social choice with respect to choosing how society allocates its resources. The problem of choice is obviously central in economic theory. The overall nature of the intended and unintended consequences of a particular economic choice is the primary concern of any theory of welfare economics. One particular welfare theory attempts to show that the unintended consequence of particular individual actions (self-interest) leads necessarily to desirable (intended?) social consequences [cf. Pigou 1962]. Arguments have arisen over which social actions lead to unintended consequences that are undesirable [cf. Arrow 1951/63, Mishan 1964] but they will not concern us here.

In the 1960s when welfare economics was a popular topic of discussion, the typical welfare analysis went as follows. If we have an economy of two persons, two scarce factors (i.e. productive resources including labour), two consumption goods (which are to be produced), then the resources will have been optimally allocated only when there is no opportunity for any person, or any producer, to gain without someone else losing. These situations are the so-called 'Pareto optima'. Usually, many such optima are possible [cf. Samuelson 1950b]. At any one of these optima each individual is choosing a combination of quantities of the two goods which maximizes his or her personal satisfaction within his or her earned income (it is assumed that such maximization is the sole intended consequence of the choice). Also, each producer is choosing the one combination of factors which maximizes its own profit within its productive constraints (it is assumed that such maximization is its sole intended consequence of its choice of productive factors). The necessary conditions for such maximization can be easily established [cf. Lerner 1944] and used as guides for (personal and public) welfare judgements. There still would remain the question of when the available resources between the two producers have been allocated optimally, which depends on whether the relative levels of satisfaction for the two persons have been optimally distributed. At least we would want the allocation to be a Pareto optimum but there may be many such possible allocations. To choose one we need a means of comparing the levels of satisfaction of the individuals concerned. Specifically, we can complete a theory of choice if we have a 'social welfare function' which would be used to evaluate each of the various allocations of resources. Since the intended social consequence of allocating resources is assumed to be to maximize social welfare, the society (by means of government action if necessary) would choose the allocation which ranks 'best' of all the possible allocations based on that social welfare function. It should be pointed out that without some sort of welfare function, the choice between Pareto optima becomes rather arbitrary.

The conventionalist's view of this social choice is to see it as an instance of the 'index number problem'. That is, the problem of computing a single number, an 'index number', which will represent (or measure) a multidimensional aggregate. This viewpoint is a 'conventionalist ploy' since it assumes the (questionable) possibility of a common measure. This conventionalist ploy has a well-known variant called 'the identification problem' which assumes the truth of a model that is used to 'identify' variables in a particular set of observations (see Chapter 3). One alternative to the conventionalist ploy is to view the choice in question as a political choice [e.g. Samuelson 1950b]. My use of welfare economics as a means of illustrating the choice problem is by no means arbitrary. As I have attempted to show elsewhere [Boland 1982, Ch. 3], there is a lot of conventionalist philosophy built into the 'problems' of economics.

The analysis of the social choice problem concerns the optimal allocation of resources that I have described so far and can be neatly represented by three interrelated diagrams [cf. Samuelson 1950b, Bator 1957]. The major ideas represented in these diagrams are as follows.

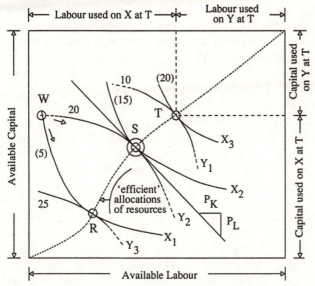

Figure 5.1 *Efficient resource allocation model*

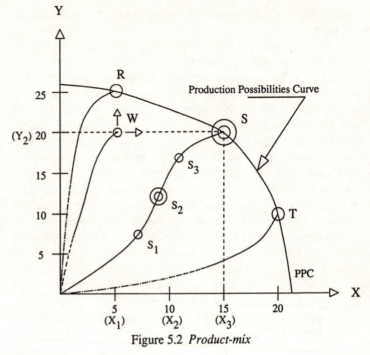

Figure 5.2 *Product-mix*

(1)   Society's resources are limited.   The limitation is represented in Figure 5.1 by a box with fixed dimensions: one side represents the available amount of labour, the other side represents the available amount of the other resource, that which we traditionally call capital. Any point in this diagram represents one allocation of these resources between the production of the two goods (**X** and **Y**).   The respective production functions are represented by two opposing sets of 'iso-quants'. Each iso-quant represents all combinations of labour and capital that will produce one level of output of a good. Given the box and the production functions, we deduce that there is a set of allocations which if any allocation is chosen, it is impossible to increase the output of one good without necessarily reducing the output of the other good (because of the scarcity implied by the fixed dimensions of the box).   This set of allocations represents all the 'efficient' allocations of the available resources. It is the locus of points of the tangency between opposing iso-quant curves that represent levels of respective outputs. In Figure 5.2 this same set of allocations is represented by possible quantities of the two goods produced. Here this set is called the Production Possibilities Curve

(PPC). Any combinations of outputs to the left or below this curve are producible with the given quantities of available resources and given technology (i.e. production functions).

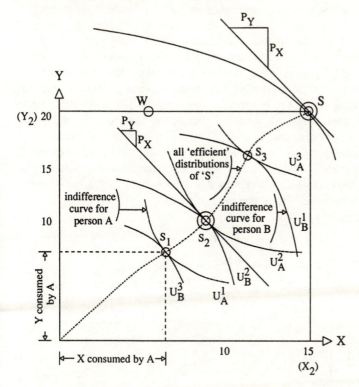

Figure 5.3 *Distribution of mix 'S'*

(2) These two diagrams are interconnected. If we happen to choose any point on the PPC in Figure 5.2, we have also implicitly chosen a point in Figure 5.1. Presumably, society in order to maximize social welfare will necessarily have to pick a point on its PPC. That is exactly what the Pareto optimum conditions assert. Moreover, all points on the PPC are potentially Pareto optima.

(3) Given that the society would want to avoid wasting its resources and thus operate its production efficiently (i.e. choose a 'product-mix' on its PPC), whether a Pareto optimum is achieved depends on how the quantities of goods produced are distributed between the two persons. In this case, we may draw a box whose dimensions are fixed by the choice of a point on PPC (see Figure

5.2 or Figure 5.3). Any point inside the box of Figure 5.3 (or Figure 5.2) represents one distribution of the available products between the two persons. We can also evaluate the various distributions by considering how the individuals evaluate them. If each individual considers combinations of goods that give the same utility to be equivalent and combinations that give more utility as better, then we can represent the implied evaluation with an iso-utility map or what is more commonly called 'an indifference map'. As with the other box (by placing one person's map starting from the lower left-hand corner and the other person's starting from the upper right-hand corner pointing downward), there is a set of efficient distributions of which if any one is chosen, it is impossible to increase one person's utility without decreasing the other's. Choosing one of these distributions is also necessary for Pareto optimality with regard to the relative distribution of utilities between individual members of society.

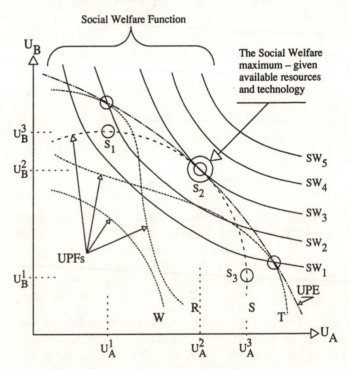

Figure 5.4 *Distributions of personal satisfaction*

(4) Given any particular choice regarding 'product-mix' there is an upper limit on both individuals' levels of utility. Analogous to the PPC of Figure 5.2, following Samuelson [1950b], this upper limit can be represented in Figure 5.4 as the Utilities Possibilities Function (UPF) where for each point on the curve representing an efficient distribution of utilities, there is one point on the locus of tangencies between opposing indifference maps. If we chose a different 'product-mix', we would generally have a different set of possible utility distributions as shown in Figure 5.4. If we consider all the possible 'product-mixes' and hence all the possible efficient allocations of resources, there is still a gross limit on all the various Utilities Possibilities Functions. This gross limit is represented by an 'envelope' which we call the Utility Possibilities Envelope (UPE). Distributions of the individuals' levels of utility on this envelope (UPE) can be reached only by choosing an allocation of resource which is efficient (i.e. producing a mix on the PPC) and choosing an optimal distribution of utilities. Furthermore, not any such optimal point will do. There will be only one such point, namely the one point on the chosen UPF which is also on the UPE.

(5) Now there are still many possible gross optimal points – i.e. Pareto optima represented by the UPE. We still need a criterion to choose between them. If we had a way of ordering all the individual distributions of utility, i.e. if we had a social welfare function such as SW in Figure 5.4 (where each curve represents a different level of social welfare), by that criterion only one such point would maximize the social welfare. In Figure 5.4 we see that the one social optimum is represented by the one distribution (S_2) on the UPE which is also on the highest iso-social welfare curve. If such a social welfare function is describable, we can thereby deduce the necessary conditions for reaching (by choice) that social optimum. Without such a function we have no reason to choose, or change, between one point on the UPE (and all its implications for resource allocations) and any other point on the UPE. However, we can give reasons for not choosing any point not on the UPE.

The question then arises: Can we ever determine such a social welfare function so as to verify the existence of a chosen social optimum? On the basis of what everyone seems to mean by an *acceptable* social welfare function, Arrow [1951/63] has 'proven' the impossibility of determining such an acceptable function. The operative concept here is the 'acceptability' of the (social welfare) function. Arrow argues that the criteria of acceptability are insufficient to rule out important logical problems of deciding unambiguously what the social welfare optimum is by any acceptable function. Note that Arrow's 'proof' does not deny the existence of a social welfare optimum, only the impossibility of rationalizing it on the basis of the 'reasonable conditions' by which the optimum is determined. A consequence of Arrow's proof is that we can never know (necessarily) when the economy has reached a social optimum, even if it has (although we may still know when it has not by showing that it has not reached at least a Pareto optimum).

The purpose of this somewhat tedious exposition is to show that welfare theory has been quite successful in working out the *criteria* for all the intermediate decisions needed to reach at least a Pareto optimum point – i.e. a point where all individual intentions are realized. Such a point is reached when all individuals are choosing combinations of goods they can afford such that they are maximizing their personal utility within the constraints of their own income. They will know they are accomplishing such maximization when the slope of their respective indifference curves equals the slope of their respective budget lines (which is determined by the market-determined relative prices). Likewise, at a Pareto optimum point each producer is choosing the combination of factor inputs such that it is maximizing its profit given the (market-determined) price of its product. The producer will know profit is maximum when the relative marginal productivity equals the (market-determined) relative prices of the factors such that costs are being minimized for the level of output.

3. Conventionalist methodological criteria

Now let me turn again to conventionalist methodology and consider the criteria used to choose one theory among competing theories. By 'competing theories' I mean only those theories which attempt to explain the same things – e.g. the traditional alternative theories of the firm (see Chapter 4). While I list here a few of the commonly suggested criteria, I want to point out that I am not trying to include all of them or even to identify particularly significant criteria. My major concern is to examine why any criterion might be seriously entertained as an essential part of a methodological study.

Suggestions concerning the choice of one theory over another include admonitions to choose the theory which is:

(a) more simple,
(b) more general,
(c) more verifiable,
(d) more falsifiable,
(e) more confirmed,
(f) less disconfirmed.

Representative examples can be found in Eddington [1958], Friedman [1953], Koopmans [1957], Poincaré [1905/52], Popper [1959/61], Samuelson [1947/65] and various essays in Krupp [1966].

For economists interested only in solving practical problems, the followers of Friedman's instrumentalism, the confirmation criterion, (e), is probably more important. Generally instrumentalists must try each theory (only) until one is found which works regardless of these criteria. Therefore I will drop further consideration of instrumentalism since it raises no interesting philosophical problems, or at least none which would interest an instrumentalist [see Boland 1979a, 1980, 1981a, 1984].

4. Choice theory in conventionalist methodology

Now I will outline a conventionalist's methodology for the choice of a theory from a set of competing theories. Let us say that with any one theory (i.e. one set of assumptions about the behaviour of people and/or institutions), say T_1, we can build many different models which differ only in how we represent each of the constituent assumptions of the theory. After specifying which variables are to be endogenous and which are to be exogenous, by specifying, say, linear behavioural relations and linear constraints, we have a model (say, M_{11}) which may be very simple but which lacks widespread applicability, i.e. generality. By increasing the number of endogenous variables (giving M_{12}) or by increasing the 'degree' of the relationships (giving M_{13}), we may build a model which is more general, but less simple. As shown in Chapter 3, changing the number of variables or the 'degree' of the relationships changes the testability of the theory. When we choose a theory we choose the things to be explained or described and thereby we face certain limits on the testability of the chosen theory. Moreover, the more we try to explain the more difficult our theory is to test (if for no other reason, we need to observe more things).

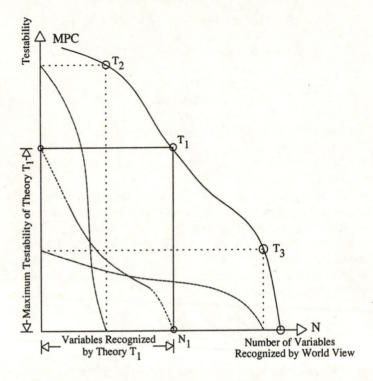

Figure 5.5 *Conceivable theories*

I have represented my understanding of models and theories with a diagram similar to the 'product-mix' diagram of welfare economics. In Figures 5.5 and 5.6 a Metaphysical Possibilities Curve (MPC) represents the limitations on possible theories within a particular 'world view', as Thomas Kuhn [1962/70] might call it. The negative slope of this curve reflects the view that as we attempt to explain more, our explanation becomes less testable.

The properties of possible models of any chosen theory are also represented within this diagram. In choosing any theory – i.e. choosing a horizontal size representing the number of variables in my diagram – there is a set of models of any particular theory which are efficient with respect to the two criteria of simplicity and generality. This set is represented by the locus of tangencies between iso-generality and iso-simplicity curves. For models off this locus it may be possible to choose other models. There may exist models off this locus which are more simple without being less general (or vice versa). This would not be possible once we have chosen a model on the locus. There may be many such 'efficient' models of a theory. The problem (of choice) is still to choose one of them.

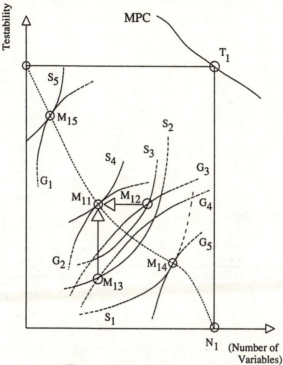

Figure 5.6 *Models of a theory*

For any theory (i.e. a set of specific models) there is an upper bound on the possible combinations of simplicity and generality. By analogy with Figure 5.4, I shall call this the Methodological Possibilities Function (MPF) and label it with the theory it represents (see Figure 5.7). Within our world view's Metaphysical Possibilities Curve, if one should choose a different theory (i.e. a different number of variables and thus a different limit on testability) one can also determine its Methodological Possibilities Function by considering all of the possible 'efficient' models of that theory.

For our current world view there are limitations on the set of all possible MPFs which are represented by the envelope of the individual MPFs. I shall call this the Methodological Frontier (MF). With this I am asserting the existence of a set of models, each of a different theory, any of which, if chosen, makes it impossible to choose another possible model or theory which has greater simplicity and no less generality (or greater generality and no less simplicity). These are, by analogy with welfare economics, the Pareto optima of our particular world view.

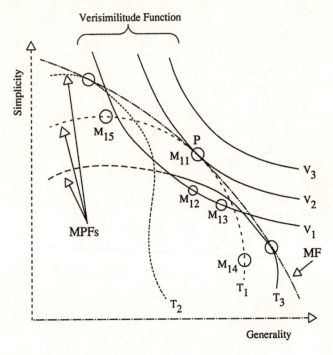

Figure 5.7 *Choice of paradigm*

The problem of choosing one of these Pareto optimal models (hence one of the theories) still remains. With the allocations of resources and distributions of personal satisfaction represented on the UPE of welfare economics (see Figure 5.4), if we do not have another means of comparing points on the UPE (e.g. if we do not have a welfare function), we cannot choose one Pareto optimum over another. In short, the criterion of Pareto optimality is necessary but not sufficient for a complete choice theory. In the case of my Methodological Frontier, in order to compare the Pareto optimal models of our world view we need another criterion in addition to those of explanatory power, simplicity, generality or testability. The most obvious criterion to use is the degree of corroboration or confirmation or what we might call a 'verisimilitude function'. The more a theory is confirmed (or confirmable because it is a good approximation), the 'better' the theory is. With such a criterion we can complete an explanation of the choice of a paradigm theory or model. Namely, we might posit that the paradigm is chosen to maximize the degree of corroboration or confirmation. I have represented this criterion in Figure 5.7 where the paradigm is the one Pareto optimal model with the highest possible degree of corroboration within our world view. Some might even say that movement towards this paradigm is 'scientific progress' and set about laying down rules (as in welfare economics) for finding it.

This then completes my presentation of the conventionalist theory choice where the choice of a theory among competing theories is based on the choice of the 'best' model within our world view. I think it is a natural outcome of the conventionalist methodology – i.e. a methodological outcome which presents methodology as a problem of choosing the 'best theory' among competing theories.

5. The failures of welfare theory

Since I want to criticize conventionalist methodology by showing, as I have, that it presents, formally, the same problem-solution situation found in welfare theory, I will now outline what I think are the major failures of welfare analysis.

(1) If we were to accept only operational definitions of a social welfare function, as Samuelson and Arrow seem to require, then we must conclude that the construction of such a welfare theory of economic choice is impossible. If Samuelson and Arrow are correct, we can never explain (within economics at least) why one Pareto optimum will be chosen over another. Those who argue this way conclude that beyond the Pareto criteria, welfare analysis is irrelevant.

(2) The problem which welfare economics seems to be solving (when we allow that social welfare functions are possible) is one of choosing between allocations of resources within the constraints of existing production technology and institutions. In other words, the problem of choice is necessarily a 'static' problem and welfare analysis is appropriately a 'static' solution. Clearly, the more interesting (and pressing) problem is to find the means of

expanding the various possibilities frontiers. Many would say that most of the economic activity in the real world seems to be directed to that problem.

(3) The welfare problem is approached as a variation of some form of a calculus problem, as a problem of maximizing some quantity (welfare). Such a view would do the job of explaining the social choice but there is no reason why every individual (let alone the society) should have a single peaked or even a monotonic welfare function. If we recognize that absence of a welfare function means that welfare does not relate to economic situations in a 'smooth and continuous way', then we must also recognize that all such forms of welfare economics fail to explain any observed social choice. Being able to draw a picture representing what we need (e.g. Figure 5.4) does not mean we are representing a realistic possibility.

6. The failures of conventionalist methodology

My critical study of conventionalist methodology is now complete. The same objections that I have listed for welfare analysis can be brought to bear against conventionalist methodology.

(1) If we accept the Popper-Socrates view that there is no operational way of knowing when a theory or model is true (even if it is true), then it is impossible to construct the necessary 'verisimilitude function' which would enable us to compare two competing theories. We may accept some econometric convention (based, for example, on R^2s, t-tests, etc.) to assign degrees of confirmation, but there is no reason why one convention would be accepted over another (unless we are only concerned with practical problems [see Agassi 1966b, 1967]). Thus the problem of choosing between theories is raised to a choice between conventions of confirmation. Thus, there is no way to resolve methodological disputes over the choice of theories on the Methodological Frontier since all theories on the Frontier are, at least, Pareto optimal by the other criteria. In the absence of a 'verisimilitude function', once we are faced with choosing between the Pareto optimal models of theories, conventionalist methodology becomes irrelevant.

(2) Philosophers such as Karl Popper [1959/61, 1965] and Joseph Agassi [1963, 1966a] have argued that conventionalist

methodology, in attempting to solve the choice problem, is pursuing an uninteresting (because unsolvable) problem. The more interesting problem might be understanding and even promoting revolutions in our world views. The efforts of science as a learning process are directed at learning through criticizing our world view, especially the limitations on our world view. Hopefully, we can expand our world view and thereby free ourselves of the constraints imposed by our current world view. This is a dynamic problem on which conventionalist methodology, even allowing for a verisimilitude function, can throw little light.

(3) Finally, as with welfare economics, the solution of the choice problems of conventionalist methodology relies on certain calculus-type situations – e.g. maximizing corroboration, maximizing expected probability, etc. To use such a method requires that the relationship between variables of a model or theory and the real world (i.e. the correspondence between theories and facts) be of a continuous, single-peaked or monotonic nature [see Boland 1986, Chs 3 and 4]. There is no reason to expect this to be the case. In fact, only one theory among *available* competitors can be true (and there is no reason why even one should be true). All others will be false. Attempts to disguise this with calculus can only increase the difficulty in criticizing our world view and thereby increase the difficulty in learning about the real world.

PART III

Exploring the Limits of the
Popper-Samuelson Demarcation

6

Uninformative Mathematical Economic Models

Anyone with the aesthetic sense to recognize the beauty of
the proof that the diagonal of a unit square is not the ratio
of two integers ... will sense the same harmony that
resides in Ricardian comparative cost or Walrasian
general equilibrium. Economic theory is a mistress of
even too tempting grace.

Paul A. Samuelson [1962/66, p. 1680]

you never get something for nothing and never empirical
hypotheses from empty deductive definitions. At best
your observation can tell you only that the real world (or
some subset of it) is not exploding; your theoretical model
or system will always be an idealized representation of the
real world with many variables ignored; it may be
precisely the ignored variables that keep the real world
stable, and it takes a significant act of inductive inference
to rule this out and permit the Correspondence Principle to
deduce properties of the idealized model.

Paul A. Samuelson [1955, p. 312]

In Chapters 2 and 3, I focused the burden of applying the Popper-
Samuelson requirement of testability on determining how many
observations it would take to refute a solution statement for any
specific model. I did not worry about how one would obtain the
needed solution statement (partly because I used primarily linear
models that easily provide solution statements). In the mid-1930s,
Abraham Wald [1936/51] examined some standard economic
models as expressed in some systems of equations. The question
he considered was whether the 'solvability' of a system of
equations used to represent a set of ideas put conditions upon the
ideas themselves. Of course, this was not merely an arithmetic
problem, as his concern was with the consistency and completeness

of the logic brought out by the use of mathematical theorems [see Boland 1970b]. The mathematics he used tended to be rather complicated and severe for the 1930s. Later developments, primarily in the 1950s, made it possible to specify the conditions for solvability in a much 'cheaper' manner [Arrow and Debreu 1954, McKenzie 1954, Gale 1955, Kuhn 1956, Nikaido 1956; see also Weintraub 1985].

The profession has moved on, confident that this matter has been settled or at least is well under control. Nevertheless, I think an important question may have been overlooked: Does solvability necessarily imply explanation? Or more generally, of what significance is the solvability of a model which represents a given explanatory theory for the given theory itself? In light of some methodological considerations concerning the reversibility of assumptions and conclusions [e.g. De Alessi 1971], it turns out that 'solvability' in a methodological context of explanation leads to undesirable (unintended) consequences. In short, solvability if properly specified leads to uninformative economic models – models which cannot say anything of empirical significance about the 'real world'.

1. A simple Walrasian general equilibrium model

Léon Walras supposedly began his famous general equilibrium analysis by putting forth a general equilibrium theory that can be represented [Dorfman, Samuelson and Solow 1958, Arrow and Hahn 1971] by the following system of equations:

$$[\Sigma] \quad \equiv \quad \begin{bmatrix} \mathbf{R} = \mathbf{A} \cdot \mathbf{X} \\ \mathbf{R} = R_0 \\ \mathbf{X} = \mathbf{D}(\mathbf{P},\mathbf{V}) \\ \mathbf{P} = \mathbf{V} \cdot \mathbf{A} \end{bmatrix}$$

where $\mathbf{X}$ is the vector indicating the quantities of $\mathbf{m}$ outputs, $\mathbf{P}$ is the vector of their prices, $\mathbf{R}$ is a vector indicating the quantities of $\mathbf{n}$ resource inputs, and $\mathbf{V}$ is the vector of the values of those inputs. Also, $\mathbf{A}$ is an $\mathbf{n} \times \mathbf{m}$ matrix of input-output coefficients and $\mathbf{D}(\ )$ is a vector formed of the appropriate $\mathbf{m}$ demand functions for the outputs.

The question that Wald could have considered is:

Does being able to solve the system of equations [Σ] for **P**, **V** and **X** imply that the system itself is an (informative) explanation of **P**, **V** and **X**?

This would, in the minds of many, raise the issue of whether the solution is a description or an explanation. Stanley Wong, in his examination of Samuelson's methodology, does just this by advocating the need for 'informative explanations' [Wong 1973, 1978]. To assist clarity, I will distinguish these concepts in the following unambiguous way:

(a)   an *informative explanation* is the 'explanation of the known by the unknown' [Popper 1972, p. 191],

(b)   a *description* is the explanation of the known by the known,

where 'explanation' is the name given to the logical relation of the explican to the explicandum [Popper 1972, p. 192] and where 'known' may be interpreted in the usual empirical sense (although it need not be restricted to that). One sense in which an explican will be an 'unknown' is when (necessarily) one of them is a strictly universal statement (e.g. 'all men are mortal'). Note that I am not equating 'explanation' with a demonstrated necessarily true explanation.

It may be that solvability will guarantee only a description but not an informative explanation. The usual position regarding the explanatoriness of a solution is that it is only a matter of logic [e.g. Debreu 1959, pp. vii-viii]. This position may be based on a popular view which simply equates explanation and description, a view attributed by Fritz Machlup [1966] to Samuelson [1963, p. 234; 1964, p. 737; see Clower and Due 1972, p. 15]. For some this is merely because 'prediction' is directly identified with 'explanation' [e.g. Marshall 1920, p. 638; Liebhafsky 1963, pp. 16-18; Ferguson 1972, p. 8]. For others this response is based on a view that economics is a 'deductive science'. Predictions or explanations are 'conditional', i.e. 'if ... then' statements [Friedman 1953, De Alessi 1965, Bear and Orr 1967, Lipsey and Steiner 1972]. This would mean that my idea of explanation only requires that the things to be explained are at least logically compatible with the reasons given. For example, Samuelson and most others would allow multiple equilibria in the explanation of some equilibrium phenomena [Samuelson 1947/65, pp. 49, 75ff, 240; Arrow and Hahn 1971, p. 15].

Wald was concerned with the question of the mathematical circumstances under which we can solve this system of equations for unique values of **P**, **V** and **X**. However, Walras' Law implies that there are only $2m+2n-1$ independent equations, so that either the uniqueness is only up to the point of relative prices, or we can add an independent equation, such as:

$$\sum_{i=1}^{m} P_i = 1$$

or merely:

$$P_1 = 1$$

which turns the relative prices into 'unique' values.

All this equation counting is of no concern here. Wald's paper began by refuting the ever-popular notion that assuring the equality between the number of independent equations and the number of 'unknowns' (i.e. endogenous variables) is necessary and sufficient to assure the existence and uniqueness of the solution of those equations. Wald went on to deal with specific representations of Walrasian theory and proved that Wald's proposed set of conditions on the **D**s and **A**s would provide the needed assurance of solvability [Wald 1936/51, Boland 1970b].

2. Methodological requirements of explanatory models

The view that explanatoriness is only a matter of logical entailments unfortunately leads to the following methodological problem over the reversal of assumptions and conclusions: What if the intended one-way relationship from a particular combination of states of **R**, **D** and **A** to a particular combination of values of **P**, **V** and **X** is logically sufficient for the relationship to also go the other way, as well? That is, what if:

$$RDA \rightarrow PVX, \text{ and } PVX \rightarrow RDA?$$

Can we consider the occurrence of a particular **PVX** to be an explanation or, within the context of the assumptions of our theory, to be 'causes' of the occurrence of the particular 'given' state of **RDA**? Surely not.

The basic idea of explanation operative in economics today has for a long time been the one based on the distinction between endogenous and exogenous variables [see Koopmans 1950b, p. 393; 1953, pp. 27, 40-4; Marschak 1953, p. 10; Hood and Koopmans 1953, p. 115]. That is, **R**, **D** and **A** influence **P**, **V** and **X** (within the model) but **R, D** and **A** are determined outside the model – i.e. **P, V** and **X** do not influence **R, D** or **A** (within the model). Although the coincidence of a particular **PVX** point with a particular **RDA** point may be interesting, it is not an explanation. As almost everyone would agree, such a circularity means that we have at best a 'pure description'. This is sometimes explicitly stated [e.g. Alchian and Allen 1967] and it is implicit in textbook discussions of the 'post hoc, ergo propter hoc' fallacy. This circularity leads to the conclusion that such reversible (complete) explanations are merely what economists usually call 'tautologies' [cf. Agassi 1971a]. When the set of conceivable **RDA**s has the same dimension as the set of conceivable **PVX**s, what I have called a pure description merely becomes a renaming routine. For example, a bundle of goods may be described by its list of goods themselves (and their quantities) or by its inherent 'characteristics' (and their quantities) following Lancaster [1966]. The matrix relating the two means of description is merely a renaming process. This placid view of complete explanation is, I think, the primary result of viewing mathematical functions as explanations.

The concept of reversibility that I have been discussing is a methodological failure if we wish to maintain the irreversibility character ascribed to the one-way influence between endogenous and exogenous variables, namely the explanatory power that results from making that distinction. It may mean that explanation is not a matter of logic alone but also involves *ad hoc* the proper use of our reversible models – i.e. the inclusion of extra *ad hoc* rules in addition to the logic of the mathematized economic models. Note, however, these needed rules are stronger than the mere 'semantic rules' discussed by linguistically oriented methodologists [see Massey 1965, p. 1159; De Alessi 1965, p. 474; cf. Simon 1953, pp. 65 and 74]. Such 'ad hocery' is quite unacceptable if we want the exogenous vs endogenous distinction to be a significant aspect of our explanations.

The irreversibility aspect of exogenous variables needs to be emphasized. It is just this condition which separates pure descriptions from explanations. This interpretation is counter to Samuelson's attempt to cast doubt on such a separation by casting doubt on one particular argument for that separation [Samuelson 1965, p. 1167]. Let us examine this separation more closely. Consider a model of our theory of explanation in which there is an intimate correspondence between mappings and explanations (see Figure 6.1). In a way, whenever the model is solvable, the Walrasian model [Σ] 'maps' from a point in the set of all conceivable combinations of Rs, Ds and As to a point in the set of all conceivable combinations of Ps, Vs and Xs. Wald's question concerns whether a unique PVX point exists for any given RDA point. With this in mind, I think economic theorists presume the following:

(1)   Explanatoriness requires that the 'mapping' be 'well defined' and 'onto'.

In mathematical economics, explanatoriness is a matter of establishing (respectively) the consistency and completeness of the model [see Boland 1970b, Wong 1973]. The mapping must be 'onto' because one has not completely explained why P, V and X are what they are unless one has also explained why they are not what they are not (relative to what is conceivable). Although this was suggested by Donald Gordon [1955a, p. 150], it is too often overlooked, even though it seems to be essential [Nikaido 1960/70, p. 268].

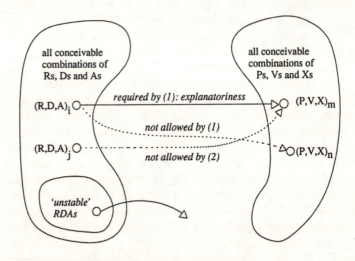

Figure 6.1 *Explaining* P, V *and* X

3. Methodological requirements of informative models

Now there is another, usually unstated, methodological requirement for any explanatory 'mapping' – we want it to be 'informative'. This is a fundamental part of the 'exogenous' character of the

RDAs and the relationships between **RDA**s and **PVX**s. These relationships are the functions to which Gordon [1955a] refers. The logic of explanation in economics is such that the postulated reasons (for why **P**, **V** and **X** are what they are) consists of the following: (a) the world operates as indicated by the assumed relationships of our model and (b) the exogenous **R**, **D** and **A** happen to be what they are. Had **R**, **D** or **A** been anything else, we would have observed different values for **P**, **V** and **X**. This then is merely a special case of a rational argument for something. The only direct test of this explanation is to determine (independently) whether the real world is as purported – i.e. whether **R**, **D** and **A** are those states which, when plugged into our model, yield the values of the **PVX** point we began with, the occurrence of which we are trying to explain [Gordon 1955a, p. 152].

Note that the common view that one tests an explanation by attempting to predict other **PVX** points on the basis of changing **R**, **D** or **A** presumes a knowledge of **R**, **D** and **A**. But, on the grounds of requirement (1) *alone*, the only means of testing the adequacy of an explanation would be to see if the representation of the explanatory mapping is well defined (and onto). That is, one would look to see if it was true that there had been a change in the **PVX** point when there was no change in the **RDA** point. If this situation were observed then one would know that their explanation of **P**, **V** and **X** is inadequate [Hansen 1970, p. 4]. The 'onto' part requires that something be said about *all* possible **PVX** points.

If requirement (1) were the only basis for a theory of explanation in economics, one could see why most economists might consider such a means of testing to be a practical impossibility in a world of exogenously changing **RDA**s. However, testing can be more than just testing the logical adequacy of the postulated reasons. Once the **RDA** point is known, we have everything needed to directly test the reasons – i.e. for the comparison of the known **RDA** point with the **RDA** point that would be logically compatible with the values of the **PVX** point we wish to explain. That **RDA** point would have to be known in order to know whether it has changed, so long as the knowledge is independent of our knowing **P**, **V** and **X**. This independence is not the case in econometrics, where we use **P**, **V**, **X**, **R** and **D** to determine what the elements of **A** are. Such considerations imply a second requirement:

(2) Informativeness (i.e. testability as falsifiability) requires the mapping to be 'one-one'.

In other words, for any **PVX** point there is only one **RDA** point which when plugged into the model yields that given **PVX** point.

4. The methodological dilemma at issue

If the mapping from **RDA**s represents the explanation of **PVX** and is, in turn, represented by a function, as would be the case with a system of equations, then that function would have to be both 'onto' and 'one-one'. This means that the function is an isomorphism, or a pure description. For our purposes, it is indistinguishable from what economists call a tautology. Moreover, such an explanation would be logically reversible hence contrary to the stated intentions [Simon 1953, p. 52]. Consequently, the methodological claim that the **PVX** point is explained (by a combination of the model and the occurrence of a particular **RDA** point) is not completely represented by the logic of the mathematized model whenever our concept of explanation must incorporate the economic theorist's desired distinction between exogenous and endogenous and still satisfy the methodological requirements of explanatoriness and testability that is found in economics literature.

Herbert Simon addressed the problem, capturing, in a non-arbitrary way, the explanatoriness of a model by analyzing the causal structure of a model. His solution was to order the equations in a chain of exogeneity whereby the endogenous variables of one equation may be exogenous to the next equation [p. 65]. Exogeneity of the entire model rested with the exogenous variables of the first equation. If we were to add Simon's needed *ad hoc* specification of one set of variables as exogenous and the remainder as endogenous, we would only beg the question that our models purport to answer.

5. The Super Correspondence Principle

The discussion so far should bring us close to the realization that the problem of explanatoriness, the problem of identification (which is usually solved by equating the number of exogenous and endogenous variables – see Chapter 3), and the problem of stability [Boland 1977b, 1986] which follows from Samuelson's 'correspondence principle' (the testability of equilibrium models requires a specification of disequilibrium dynamics that would provide an explanation for why the equilibrium state was achieved) are not separate issues as most economic theorists would seem to think.

Rather, these three allegedly separate problems are all variants of one methodological problem – namely, the problem of the informativeness (beyond available data) of our economic theories and models. No one of the allegedly separate problems is solved unless all of them are solved. It is what might be called the *Super Correspondence Principle*.

The informativeness of the explanation of **PVX** would be assured when it is realized that the stability analysis of a model must allow for some **RDA**s for which there does not exist 'equilibrium' **PVX**s. That is, the set of conceivable (independently of the given theory) combinations of **R**s, **D**s and **A**s must contain at least one subset of combinations which do not 'map' to any **PVX** point. On the basis of an independent concept of **R**, **D** or **A** (specifically, one which does not assume that the given theory of **PVX** is true), unless it is logically possible to identify conceivably observable **RDA** combinations which would imply 'unstable' or inconsistent circumstances for the determination of the **PVX**s, there is no assurance that anything has been explained.

6. Falsifiability to the rescue

Such a consideration leads to the addition of an extra clause to requirement (2) – namely, the empirical falsifiability requirement that there are points in the **RDA** set which do not map into the **PVX** set. With this addition the requirement now is that the independently conceivable data will not only contain counter-examples (false 'if-then' predictions) but will necessarily extend beyond what could be known from the observance of confirming data (true 'if-then' predictions).

Two things should be noted. The first is simple: Any *ad hoc* specification of exogeneity to some particular variables will not be equivalent to the addition of the extra clause to requirement (2) as the latter cannot be satisfied *ad hoc* but must be done *within* the theory of **PVX**. The second is more important: Once the extra clause is added to requirement (2), mathematical models consisting only of functional relationships will never be able to satisfy the augmented second requirement. This is because any function which is 'well defined', 'onto' and 'one-one' will imply the existence of the unique inverse, which is itself such a function. That would mean that the inverse is 'onto', which is a direct contradiction of the extra clause. Note that by defining **RDA** such that it is consistent with all **PVX**s, the 'explanation' is rendered uninformative since the theory would be circular and the circularity implies the reversibility of assumptions and conclusions.

In conclusion, I note that Wald and those mathematical economists who followed him were concerned with the mathematical requirements of solvability of mathematized economic models but may have failed to see the problem in the context of a complete theory of explanation which is able to distinguish explanations from descriptions or other pure exercises in logic. As a result, the common presupposition that explanation is a matter of logic alone leads to the view that 'a superior description ... can be given the honorific title of "explanation"' [Samuelson 1965, p. 1171] even though such a view contradicts the ordinary economic theorist's rationale for distinguishing between exogenous and endogenous variables.

7

On the Impossibility of Testability
in Modern Economics

> to test, refute, or 'verify' a meaningful proposition is a
> tough empirical job and no amount of flossy deduction
> can obviate this.
> Paul A. Samuelson [1955, pp. 310-11]

> The only point that can be affirmed with confidence is that
> a model for a theory is not the theory itself.
> Ernest Nagel [1961, p. 116]

Philosophers of science have drawn fine distinctions between the
ideas of testability, falsifiability, verifiability, refutability, and the
like, but little of their literature seems relevant for economists.
Economists today rarely make much of a distinction between testability and falsifiability (or refutability). Following Samuelson
[1947/65], and bolstered by Popper [1959/61], in recent times the
economics profession seems to have adopted one particular view of
the philosophy of science to the exclusion of all other views.

The philosopher Karl Popper and the economic theorist Paul
Samuelson have made falsifiability the keystone of their respective
philosophies of science. Popper tells us that a theory is 'scientific
only if it is capable of being *tested* by experience' [1959/61, p. 40].
However, Popper argued that, as a matter of logic, testability
cannot be verifiability. Specifically, verification, the demonstration of the truth of a statement or theory, is impossible any time we
have to prove that a *strictly universal* statement is true – *even if it is
true* [p. 70]. For example, in proving that *'all* swans are white' we
must guarantee that no future swan will be non-white. This
consideration does not preclude falsifiability, as one can prove that
such a statement is false with the demonstration of one or more
counter-examples [p. 69, see Chapter 2 above]. Samuelson is more

direct as he claims that a scientific theory must be empirically falsifiable [1947/65, p. 14; 1953, p. 1]. So both Popper and Samuelson use empirical falsifiability as a demarcation criterion to identify scientific theories.

The foundation of Popper's logical view of testability is the elementary asymmetry recognized in ordinary quantificational logic [Quine 1965]. Specifically, there is an asymmetry between the testability of statements which use the universal quantifiers 'all' or 'every' and the testability of those which use the existential quantifiers 'some' or 'at least one'. This *quantificational asymmetry* will be fundamental in the view to be examined here. The principle concern will be the view that in economics we must be concerned to put forth statements or theories which, as Samuelson [1947/65, p. 4] says, 'could conceivably be refuted, if only under ideal conditions'. As we shall see, Popper's logic sword cuts both ways when we build *models* of our theories.

I think it is important to recognize that, contrary to the popular perception of proponents of 'falsificationism' [e.g. Blaug 1980], testability is more often demanded by 'verificationists' than by 'Popperians' who supposedly demand 'falsifiability' as opposed to 'verifiability'. One would not want to waste time trying to verify a tautology, would one?[1]

When ordinary economists promote the requirement of testability, their purpose is not always obvious. Does testability of a theory mean that it is conceivably false (thus, not a tautology) or that it is conceivably falsifiable (thus, it is possible for the real world to be so constructed that some possible observation would contradict the theory *as a whole*) or does it mean something else?

In this chapter, I examine the basis for testability in modern economics where testability is to be viewed as the possibility of *empirical refutation*, that is, the possibility of observing conceivable facts which when conjoined with the theory in question forms a logical contradiction. This chapter is intended to

---

1   However, the economic theorist Cliff Lloyd held that falsifiability is necessary but not sufficient for testability [Lloyd 1969, p. 87]. Some Popperians, however, do not always relate testability so strongly with falsifiability, as this distinction seems to involve extra-logical matters such as the purposes for testing. For example, Kurt Klappholz and Joseph Agassi [1959, p. 65] argued that 'Tests can easily be performed without risk of falsification...; but nothing can be learnt from such testing'. This latter distinction will not be the issue here. Nor will the weaker view of testability which only requires that data deducible from a theory be 'comparable' with empirical evidence [cf. Archibald 1966].

challenge those economists who would have us utter nothing but testable (empirically refutable) statements *and* who also put a premium on logical arguments. The examination is concerned with two basic questions: (1) When is a statement (e.g. prediction or assumption) considered to be false? And (2) when is a theory as a whole considered to be false?

The discussion will focus exclusively on the now common view which presumes that one tests a theory by building a representative model of it and then tests that model. My argument will be an outline of a proof that it is impossible to test convincingly any economic theory if only models of the theory are tested (this proof will hold even when the theory is not tautological). The basis for the proof will be (a) the common presumption that a test of a model representing a theory constitutes a test of that theory (i.e. nothing more is required), (b) the methodological role of models (i.e. they involve additional assumptions in order to test a theory), (c) the rather standard view of testing (i.e. tests are always relative to testing conventions), and (d) the nature of logic (i.e. it is ambiguous regarding which assumption 'causes' a false prediction).

Economics today is thought to be capable of being 'scientific' mainly because economic theorists now have accepted the need to express their ideas in terms of specific models [see Sassower 1985, Ch. 2]. Mathematical models of economic theories supposedly have enabled us to perform tests of economic theories. The central question of this chapter is: Does refuting a specific model of a given theory *necessarily* refute the theory represented by that model? If not, then the popular methodological requirement that our theories be testable would seem to be rather puzzling at best. It will be argued here that for fundamental logical reasons it is impossible to test an economic theory by constructing specific *models* of that theory which are more empirically restrictive than the theory itself.

1. Tautology vs testability

Despite Samuelson's 1955 warning, little has been said in our literature that examines the logic of testing in economics. A possible exception is Bear and Orr [1967], but even their examination was limited to the discussion surrounding Friedman's instrumentalistic view concerning the need to test assumptions [Friedman 1953, see also Boland 1979a].

As I have briefly noted above, the current positive concern for testability may stem instead from the older methodological prescription that we should strive to verify our theories, assumptions or predictions. The problem that might face any theorist or model builder is that a tautology could be 'verified' even though one might think it is not meaningful or informative. That is, a successful verification might not be meaningful. To assure that any verification is meaningful one should make sure one's theories are not tautologies. On the other hand, if a theory is testable then any verification would be meaningful. This prescription persists despite the above noted methodological arguments which seem to undermine the possibility of a successful verification of a testable (non-tautological) theory by showing that such a verification would go beyond what is empirically possible.

The requirement of testability has survived because most model builders presume it to be the sole means of avoiding tautologies. Actually, to avoid tautologies, all we need do is establish that our theories are conceivably false [Samuelson 1947/65, pp. 4, 22 and 172]. Testability may be a stronger requirement if viewed only from the basis of the logical properties of a theory. It has been argued that any statement which is conceivably falsifiable is, by logical necessity, testable since a counter-example which would falsify the theory could quite well be viewed as the outcome of a successful test [Finger 1971]. I have argued elsewhere that in economics (though perhaps not in physics) testability is quite different from conceivable falsifiability [Boland 1977b] but it is best to leave all such sophistication aside for the present.

2. Test criteria as conventions

Given that it is not always clear what ordinary economists mean by testability, as a first step in my argument against the possibility of direct model-based testability in modern economics, I wish to consider a distinction between testability and falsifiability. Falsification is a logical property of *successful* tests [Popper 1959/61, pp. 32-3] although it is not exclusive to them. A falsification is a proof that a statement in question is false. The primary logical aspect of a test is setting up a situation where the conjunction of what is being tested and the frame of reference against which it is being tested either yields a logical contradiction or it does not [see Boland 1983]. It would be ideal if that frame of reference were indisputable facts or observations, such that the proof of falsity would be beyond question and hence absolute. But few of us would adopt such a naive view today. It is this non-existence of absolute facts which leads us to distinguish between testing and falsification. Testing itself is a willful act, one for which there are problems that extend beyond the logical question of falsification. Testing (at least today) is done in a manner designed to convince someone else (perhaps one's colleagues) of the truth or falsity of a particular theory of some type.[2] When testing and falsification are not considered identical, it is not uncommon to find that what distinguishes testing from purely logical falsification is that testing, in any allegedly scientific enterprise such as economics, is a 'sociological' problem – a matter of social conventions [e.g. Lloyd 1965, p. 20; Blaug 1968, p. 7]. So, to keep things clear I will say that falsification is considered to be absolute whereas a test is relative to the testing standards agreed on (i.e. the criteria and the frame of reference).[3]

Problems could arise if we accept this distinction between falsification and testing. Whenever a social agreement *alone* must be relied on for testing conventions we must, logically, allow for any arbitrary convention [Lloyd 1969, p. 89] but this might also allow for possible dishonesty or 'self-interested phantasies' [Zeuthen 1957, p. 6]. To avoid the possibility of dishonesty we could revert to requiring absolute logical proofs of any falsification of a test statement (even when it is only within the relative context of the accepted conventions) [Lloyd 1965, p. 23]. This, however, leads to an infinite regress as every logical proof must itself use some assumptions. Thus the proof can be questioned, and the proof of the proof can be questioned, and so on. Testing as a sociological problem would seem to mean that we must choose between a dangerous arbitrariness or a hopeless infinite regress.

If the famous historian of science, Thomas Kuhn, is correct, the existence of a community of scientists seems to create another option. Any logical proof of falsification of a test statement is considered relative to the accepted 'world view' as manifested in our revealed 'paradigms' [Kuhn 1962/70]. The paradigms are the pool of available assumptions used to construct the logical proof of

---

2 Most practical 'testing' today is done in the context of 'safeguards' for society against dangerous drugs, building techniques, etc. This concept of testing easily applies to economic policy – but this, too, is not the use of testing that concerns us here because that is not what theorists such as Samuelson discuss.

3 An example would be an acceptable definition of a 'swan' or a 'firm', or an acceptable statistical parametric indicator [cf. Lloyd 1965, p. 23].

any falsification. They are the basis of our test conventions and are at any present moment – during everyday workings of 'normal science' – considered beyond question. Benjamin Ward [1972], for example, identifies 'liberal philosophy' as the basic paradigm of neoclassical economic theory. The famous 'impossibility proof' of Kenneth Arrow [1951/63] is based on unquestioned assumptions that are fundamental to that 'liberal philosophy'. The acceptance of the paradigms stops the potential infinite regress. This philosophical strategy is sometimes called 'Fideism' [see Bartley 1964b]. At the same time, the acceptance hopefully avoids the two problems of subjective truth – namely dishonesty and self-delusion. The avoidance is possible because the criteria are slowly developed within the community and only with ample support of the entire community of scientists are they still applied [Kuhn 1962/70, Ward 1972].

Which philosopher or historian of science is quoted to support one's preconceptions of methodology in economics is usually a fad but it is safe to assume for the purposes of this discussion that Kuhn's view of science comes closest to representing what is commonly accepted and practised in economics. On this basis we can say that a false test statement (e.g. a prediction) is one which contradicts the 'facts' as defined by our 'world view' (i.e. our paradigms). To many this would seem to be the only way we can define 'false' and avoid the above problems. Within this context (i.e. Fideism) a successful test can be convincing since the basis for the logical proof is, by common agreement, considered beyond question for the immediate purposes (i.e. normal science). Our 'world view' thus becomes our needed frame of reference – the starting or stopping point of *all* rational arguments. The danger for the would-be methodologist here is that 'theories' might be confused with 'world view' [cf. Weintraub 1985]. Equating the 'world view' with our theories would turn all of economics into a tautology [see Agassi 1971a]. That is, if our basic theories are beyond question – because they are treated as paradigms – there would be nothing to test. The fact that we consider alternative theories (of the firm or of the consumer) means that the standard theory is *not* a paradigm – no matter how standard. To identify our 'world view' we must look much deeper into such things as our ideas of individualism [Simon 1963, p. 230; Ward 1972, p. 26; Boland 1982, Ch. 2], of the independence of decision-making [Morgenstern 1972, p. 1171; Ward 1972, p. 26; Boland 1977b] or even the inherent goodness of Pareto optimality [Morgenstern

1972, p. 1169]. Of course, the details of our 'world view' are not the issue here, only the recognition that such a view exists.

3. The role of logic in testing

Both falsification and successful testing depend on logical proofs of some kind. Before we get to the matter of the role of logic, let us examine the nature of ordinary logic. Beyond our conventions concerning the criteria by which we would agree that a given test statement is false and constrained by the quantificational asymmetry noted above, testing relies on some important asymmetrical properties of logic [e.g. Bear and Orr 1967, p. 190]. These properties follow from the construction of our standard logic. We can say, for a given *set* of premises from which a set of conclusions is said to follow logically, that:

(1) if *all* the premises are true (in some sense) then *all* the conclusions will be true (in the same sense), without exception; and its corollary,

(2) if *any* conclusion is false (not true by the same sense) then *at least one* premise *of the given set* is false – but we do not know which premise is false (when there is more than one) nor do we know how many are false, for they could all be false;

(3) if any premise is false, it does not preclude any of the conclusions from being true; and its corollary,

(4) if any one of the conclusions is true, any of the premises from the given set could still be false.

Truth here is a property of a statement. A statement can be true or false. Truth is not something that can be discussed separately from the statement which exhibits the truth status in question. Nevertheless, it is heuristically useful to pretend that it is a quantity that can be passed around. In this (and only in this) heuristic sense we can say that if logic is correctly applied, the truth of the premises (or assumptions) will be 'passed' on to the conclusions (or predictions). However, even when correctly applied, the truth of the conclusions cannot usually be 'passed' back to the premises. Consequently, there is an asymmetry between the directions of apparent transfer. It is also true of this asymmetrical property that the falsity of the conclusions can be 'passed' back at least to the set of premises, but the falsity of the premises is in no way 'passed' to the conclusions (except those conclusions identical to the false premises). A more subtle asymmetry can be pointed out: whereas the truth of the *set* of premises is 'passed' unambiguously to *every* conclusion, the falsity of *any one* conclusion is 'passed' ambiguously only to the *set* of premises; that is, not necessarily to any particular premise. (All this is said with the realization that the truth of our theory is a separate matter from the knowledge of that truth – which is another asymmetry [see Boland 1982, Ch. 11; 1986, p. 18].)

There does not seem to be any significant dispute about these asymmetries. The consequences of these facts about logic define the role of logic in testing. First, it is impossible to verify a *theory* by examining only the conclusions that may be deduced from it (even though we may show many of them to be true). Second, it is impossible to verify any of the conclusions *indirectly* from the *known* truth of all the premises whenever any one of the premises of the theory happens to be a strictly universal statement (as at least one must be, in order for the theory to explain or predict [Popper 1959/61, p. 60]). As I noted already, this is so merely because we can never *know* when a strictly universal statement is true in terms of empirical facts from which that knowledge is alleged to follow logically. And third, showing any premise to be false says nothing about the truth or falsity of the conclusions.[4] The inability to pin down the source of falsity (of a conclusion) in the *set* of premises, i.e. property (2), is probably *the* major obstacle in testing economic theories. A falsification of one conclusion (e.g. a prediction) need not say much about the theory *if* additional assumptions have been added to the theory to make it testable.[5] Since this is exactly what we do when we build a *model* (see Chapter 1), we need to examine the consequences of using the asymmetries of logic somewhat more closely.

4. The role of models in testing theories

As I noted in Chapter 1, there are two main reasons economists might wish to test their behavioural theories. Applied economists might wish to test for the limits of applicability of their general

---

4 An exception is the trivial case pointed out by Samuelson [1963] where the purpose of a set of assumptions is to form a pure description.

5 An exception is the rare case where the *only* additional assumptions were paradigmatic and beyond question [see Boland 1981b].

theories. Pure theorists might wish to determine the truth status of their theories. In economics, theories are made empirically testable by constructing models of our theories [e.g. Marschak 1953, p. 25; Koopmans 1957, p. 173; Papandreou 1958, pp. 8-11; Arrow 1968, p. 639]. As I have tried to show in Chapters 2 and 3, as well as Chapter 6, how one chooses to build a specific model can have profound consequences for the testability of the constructed model. In those chapters we were dealing with only non-stochastic models. Here the discussion is more general. Nevertheless, the essential point is that models are constructed to be more specific than the behavioural theories they represent.

One way to test the limits of applicability of a theory is to apply that theory to a practical real-world situation. Practical real-world situations are very specific. For example, demand elasticities may be known in advance, production cost functions may be easy to specify. With such considerations in mind, it is possible to build a model of a theory that is limited to a specific situation, in the sense that there is no claim that it would pass a test when applied to some other situation with different demand elasticities or cost functions.

Those theorists concerned with the truth status of their theories also build specific models when performing empirical tests. To be specific enough for the purposes of an empirical test (that is, with evidence drawn from the real world), it is almost always necessary to modify the general behavioural theory with extra assumptions (as is routinely done in econometric tests) by representing the behavioural situation with specific mathematical functions [Koopmans 1953, p. 29]. Should the production function be linear or quadratic or what? Should we worry about formal solutions that imply negative output levels when none will ever be observed? Recognizing that there may be random errors in the observations used to construct the test, what is the allowable error in a statement of equality implied by an explicit equation? Such questions must be addressed when building a specific model of a theory whether our objectives are those of applied theorists concerned with the applicability of their theories or of pure theorists concerned with the question of whether their theories constitute true explanations of the economy. To answer these questions is to specify the additional assumptions.

The central question for the theorist who builds models to test the truth status of a theory (or to test the theory's applicability) concerns the well-known 'problem' that follows from the ambiguity caused by the addition of the assumptions needed to specify the model. If a model is revealed to be false by a test, does this mean that the theory it represents is false or that it is just a poor representation? To deal with this question, I would like to make clear the ingredients of a model. Initially, I wish to recognize two separate ingredients: the theory itself and the added assumptions used to specify the functions that represent the theory. This gives the following schemata for the concept of a model as used here:

(A) A *set of behavioural assumptions* about people and/or institutions. This set might include, for example, the behavioural proposition $C = f(Y)$, where $\partial C / \partial Y$ is positive. The *conjunction* of all the behavioural assumptions is what traditionally constitutes a 'theory'.

(B) A *set of simplifying assumptions* about the relationships contained in the above set. For example, the demand function stated in the theory might be specified as a linear function, $C = a + bY$, where a is positive and b is between 0 and 1.

Any model is a conjunction of these two sets of assumptions. The schemata lists these sets in a descending order of autonomy. As discussed in Chapter 2, the nature of the assumptions about functional forms is limited by the number of relevant variables recognized in the theory. And, as discussed in Chapter 3, an econometric study presumes that the two sets of assumptions are true and applies them to actual data to deduce the parametric values recognized by the second set.

That a model is a conjunction of more than just an explanatory theory means that from consideration (2) of the asymmetries of logic (see Section 3, p. 135), we must conclude that when a prediction of a model is falsified we still do not know specifically whether the 'cause' was a basic assumption of the theory or an additional assumption introduced in the model's construction [Lloyd 1965, p. 22]. This is an important consideration for all those who say that the purpose of constructing mathematical models of a theory is to *make* that theory testable.

5. The falsification of theories using models

Now we are close to establishing the major point of this chapter. If we think we are going to test an unspecified theory by showing that it is false on the basis of empirical tests, then we must be prepared

138

to be able to show that all possible models of the theory are false. In other words, to test the basic behavioural assumptions themselves we must consider all possible ways of modelling them (however simple or complex). Unfortunately, this is a very difficult assignment since there will always be an infinite number of ways of modelling any given theory. In the absence of errors in logic, if *every* one of the modelling assumptions when conjoined with the basic assumptions can be shown to lead to *at least one* false prediction then at least one basic assumption must be false. And if that were not the case, that is if all the assumptions are (non-tautologically) true, then it is *possible* to specify the basic assumptions such that no false predictions could or would ever happen. I wish to stress that I am making this argument without having to resort to extraordinary or otherwise severe concepts of truth and falsity. To the contrary, my argument here presumes that the determination of the truth of any prediction is a matter of ordinary testing conventions (e.g. R^2 of appropriate value) which, as noted in Section 2, need only be consistent with the accepted 'world view' of the community of scientists.

Obviously, the requirement that we must show that *all* possible models are false is impossible – for the same reason that it is impossible to verify a strictly universal statement (the quantificational asymmetry). We must therefore conclude that on this basis (i.e. the relative basis of our 'world view') *the empirical falsification (and thus testability) of any economic theory is impossible whenever the test is based only on an evaluation of models representing the theory*. For future reference I will call this the Ambiguity of Direct Model Refutation. It is also obvious that we cannot have the ability to do something which is impossible. So, the Ambiguity of Direct Model Refutation means that any economists who say that falsifiability is necessary but not sufficient for testability may have to admit to the impossibility of testability in modern economics.

6. The 'bad news'

It is always very difficult to write about methodology. Even if one were to prove that positive supporting evidence in no way decides the truth of a theory, readers will still demand positive evidence of one's proof. Methodologists are not immune to such inconsistencies.

This chapter was motivated partly by the popularity among economists of the view that our major methodological concern is, and should be, the testability of our theories. (I have heard of more than one theoretical manuscript being rejected by editors because it could not be shown that it contributed to an increase in the testability of standard demand theory.) Increased testability is, by implication, the primary criterion of scientific progress.

I have deliberately referred to very few examples in this chapter because I think the possibility of direct testability is a matter of logical inconsistency. Besides, one cannot prove impossibility with a long list of examples. The view that one must show an example of an error to show that an error of logic exists is itself an error of logic! I am concerned with the logic of the commonplace *argument* for testability in economics. It is sufficient to show that a logical error exists. Note that by property (2) of logic (p. 135), showing one conclusion (or prediction) to be false indicates that one (or more) of the assumptions is false *but that condition presumes the absence of logical error*.

In summary, the foregoing constitutes a theory of testing in modern economics. It is based on: (1) the asymmetries of logic which are beyond question here, (2) the assumption that economists are followers of something like Kuhn's view of science at least to the extent that the acceptance of test results depends on the use of conventionally accepted test criteria, and (3) the empirical assumption that economists think their theories are not directly testable except by constructing (mathematical) *models of their theories*. It is logically impossible to combine these assumptions with the Popper-Samuelson doctrine that we must utter only testable economic statements. What are we to do? Perhaps all economists interested in scientific rigour need to examine their view that testability is the sole means of avoiding tautologies. There simply are more ways than one to avoid tautologies. In short, on the safe assumption that we are unwilling to abandon ordinary logic, we may have to yield either to the falsity of the strategy of relying on Kuhn's view of science which presumes that testing must be based only on socially accepted testing conventions (see Chapter 5) or to the falsity of Samuelson's methodology which avoids tautologies only by requiring testability – or to the falsity of both.

8

Model Specifications, Stochasticism and Convincing Tests in Economics

> Refutations have often been regarded as establishing the failure of a scientist, or at least of his theory. It should be stressed that this is an inductivist error. Every refutation should be regarded as a great success; not merely a success of the scientist who refuted the theory, but also of the scientist who created the refuted theory and who thus in the first instance suggested, if only indirectly, the refuting experiment.
>
> Karl R. Popper [1965, p. 243]

> Even in the most narrowly technical matters of scientific discussion economists have a shared set of convictions about what makes an argument strong, but a set which they have not examined, which they can communicate to graduate students only tacitly, and which contains many elements embarrassing to the official rhetoric. A good example is the typical procedure in econometrics.
>
> Donald N. McCloskey [1983, p. 494]

There are two basic problems relating to discussions of methodology. Too much is taken for granted and too little has been worked out with the thoroughness we have come to expect in discussions of other aspects of economics. Throughout this book I have attempted to analyze critically the explicit process of building models of our traditional economic theories. Model building is so widely practiced in economics that it becomes very difficult to question the soundness of the process. Even when we accept the traditional theories of the textbooks we still must make decisions regarding the process of applying them to the real world. As such the process of model building is certainly not automatic. There may be infinitely many potential models that could be used to represent any given theory. However, it does not matter whether we view model building as a process of choosing between existing complete models or a process of building from the ground up, so to speak, assumption by assumption.

In Chapters 6 and 7, I have dealt with specific problems that arise in the process of model building, problems which are peculiar to models and to their relationship with the given theory. The question 'What is the purpose for building any model?' must always be asked. No single model will serve all purposes. The models we build to describe or explain the real world will not necessarily be usable for testing the given theory. Similarly, models built for quick application to policy issues may not always be sufficiently realistic for plausible explanations or convincing tests.

Sometimes one might suspect that these considerations may not be well understood or appreciated by most economists. Too often it is assumed that a model which has been shown to be successful for one purpose (e.g. description of data) will automatically be sufficient for another (e.g. testing). Throughout this chapter, I will be examining two specific types of erroneous methodological positions often taken regarding testing and the nature of models. The first position is the one taken by economists who claim to have performed tests of economic theories by testing models whose specifications represent 'interpretations' of those theories. More is required than testing numerous models or interpretations of those theories. The second popular position is the one which views the real world as a necessarily 'stochastic environment'. The problem here is that it is our models which are stochastic rather than the world we wish to explain.

1. Falsifiability lives in modern economics

Critics of Popper's philosophy of science or Samuelson's methodology were probably encouraged in Chapter 7 by my pessimistic look at the possibility of refuting a theory by testing only a model of that theory. Many of Popper's critics will continue to argue that in actual practice ordinary economists do not refute their theories. Refutability, the critics might say (in concert with Chapter 5), is a conventionalist criterion for theory choice and any progress in economics has not been due to economists refuting their theories and replacing them by better ones – that is, by economists practicing what the critics call Popper's 'falsificationism' (e.g.

Daniel Hausman, Wade Hands, Bruce Caldwell, etc.). Economic methodologists who may be so eager to dismiss Popper's view of science are unable to see the forest for the trees. Perhaps they spend too much time talking to philosophers rather than to practicing economists.

Modern economics is characterized more by the activities of model builders than by debates among economic philosophers and ideologists. Modern economists see themselves engaged in an ongoing saga of advances in model building. The behavioural theory that ordinary economists attempt to model has not changed in several decades, but various models come and go. Roy Weintraub [1985, pp. 112-17 and 121] argues eloquently in his history of neo-Walrasian economics that there was steady progress from the 1930s to the high plateau in the work of Arrow and Debreu [1954] which continues to be refined even today. What I have been calling the set of behavioural assumptions is what Weintraub and others call the 'core' or 'hard core' of a research programme. He said that there has been significant progress in the 'hardening of the hard core'. The hardening is a result of the axiomatization of general equilibrium theory followed by a long series of adjustments to the list of behavioural assumptions. The adjustments have been primarily ones which reduce the list to just those necessary and sufficient to represent any Walrasian general equilibrium.

Critics of neoclassical economics may wish to say that measuring the extent to which the core has been hardened sometimes requires a powerful microscope. The progress in general equilibrium theory is much more visible when it is seen to involve the rejection (rather than empirical refutation) of various modelling techniques. In the 1930s the use of calculus-based techniques were commonplace. The utility or production functions were specified to be everywhere continuous and differentiable in order to complete a model of general equilibrium. The functions were specified as such to fulfill the requirements of Brouwer's fixed point theorem which was commonly used to prove the existence of a general equilibrium [see Wald 1936/51]. Calculus was eventually rejected as a basis of general equilibrium modelling. In later models the continuous utility and production functions were replaced with 'upper semi-continuous' set-theoretic correspondences. These less demanding specifications were allowed by Kakutani's fixed point theorem [see Debreu 1959]. The testing standards – if we wish to see the process in these terms – were the criteria employed by formalist mathematicians. Any model which cannot be shown to meet the 'standards of rigor of the contemporary formalist school of mathematics' [Debreu 1959, p. viii] is to be rejected in the same way empirical models are rejected when they do not meet the standards set by the currently accepted testing conventions.

As I have noted in Chapter 1, economists today are more concerned with testing models than testing theories. Models are routinely rejected without ever calling into question the basic set of behavioural assumptions or ever seeing a need for adjustments [see Boland 1981b]. The linear algebra of activity analysis and linear programming used extensively during the 1950s and 1960s has virtually disappeared from the literature. Game theory was briefly popular in the 1960s and seems to have reappeared in the 1980s. None of the changes in modelling techniques has resulted in changes in the basic behavioural assumptions.

Editors of the **Journal of Political Economy** and the **Journal of Money, Credit, and Banking** have often complained that failed attempts to fit data have not been reported. The problem, as these complaints imply, is that the actual refutations of models and modelling techniques are not observable phenomena. I think the widespread practice of simply not reporting failed empirical models has misled the critics of Popper to think that falsificationism is unrealistic. Certainly, the rejection of linear models in favour of quadratic models implies that some economists consider linear models of certain phenomena to be false. Similarly, if we go beyond Chapter 7 by recognizing that any chosen estimation convention is an integral part of one's econometric model [see Boland 1977a] then we can also see that economists who reject ordinary least-squares (OLS) in favour of generalized least-squares (GLS) or two-stage least-squares (2SLS) as means of estimating a model's pa.ameters do so because they have found models based on OLS estimates to be false in some important respect. Of course, there are many unreported models which researchers have deemed false and thus unusable for the purpose of model building. These observations lead me to conclude that if we view the practice of economics to be building and testing models rather than the more lofty pursuit of testing general theories of economics, then falsification lives regardless of the views of some critics of Popper's philosophy of science.

2. Overcoming Ambiguity of Direct Model Refutations

Through the eyes of practicing economists it is easy to see that the critics of Popper's so-called falsificationism are wrong. Ordinary practicing economists, who see their task as one of building and applying models of neoclassical economics, will testify that the occurrence of *model* refutation is a common experience. Nevertheless, spending one's time refuting particular models without ever addressing the question of testing neoclassical theory itself seems less than satisfactory. Surely one can go beyond the problems inherent in the Ambiguity of Direct Model Refutation. In the remainder of this chapter I present an approach to testing which to some extent does overcome the Ambiguity of Direct Model Refutation. For anyone trying to refute a theory it will require a little extra effort before they rush off to employ the latest modelling techniques.

2.1. Critical interpretations are merely models

Our central concern in Chapter 7 was the issue of testing with models. In this context, I argued only that the falsification of a model of a theory does not necessarily imply the falsification of the theory itself and I called this the Ambiguity of Direct Model Refutation. The methodological problem at issue concerned the logical relationship between models and theories and the limitations imposed by the principles of ordinary logic. In this light I noted that all testing involves adding extra assumptions to the theory being tested. That is, it involves building a model of the theory in order to test the theory. Surely, one cannot expect to be able to observe just one false model and thereby prove the theory itself to be false. If one thinks that theories are refutable in this way, then one's job would appear to be much too easy. For example, one could always append a known false extra assumption to a theory and thereby construct a model which is automatically false. Certainly, such testing would be 'unfair' at best. Just as surely we would have no reason to expect that proponents of a theory would accept such a 'refutation' of their theory. So, in what way does building a model of a theory constitute a test *of the theory*?

Many economists seem to think that the act of building a model always constitutes a test of a theory because the act of specification amounts to an interpretation of the theory. For example, in a critique of Milton Friedman's famous essay on methodology, Tjallings Koopmans claimed that if any one interpretation of a theory is false then the theory must be false [Koopmans 1957, p. 138]. This method of criticism presumes that 'interpretation' is a process equivalent to a logical derivation from a set of given postulates without the addition of any other assumptions. Probably only mathematicians would make such a claim since the pure mathematical models used by economists are always presumed to be logically complete. With complete models, the only possibility of a false interpretation would be due to an error in the logical derivation. Surely, there are other ways to produce a false interpretation. If so, under what circumstances does a possibly false interpretation of someone's view constitute a criticism of that view?

Despite Koopmans's presumption, the ordinary sense of the word 'interpretation' (like 'model building') always involves additional assumptions (e.g. 'I assume by this word you mean ...'). Moreover, any assumption could be false. Putting numbers in place of letters in mathematical models is an overt act of 'specifying' the equations. Most interpretations require such specifications of the variables. Such specification involves at least an assumption about their dimension or scale and this type of specification, too, involves possibly false assumptions. In other words, a model is merely a mode of interpretation. More important, a model or an interpretation can lead to a successful direct criticism (or test) only when what has been added is known to be true. This is the root of the problem. Testing a theory by adding assumptions and finding that the resulting model does not 'fit the facts' does not usually allow us to conclude that the theory was at fault since our added assumptions may not be true.

Some readers may say that the real root of this problem is that it is always difficult or impossible to determine when any assumption is true. They may be right and I will consider how model builders cope with this question. First, let us assume that it is possible to make true observations such that there is no ambiguity concerning whether a model 'fits the facts', so that I can show that testing theories with models is not completely impossible. The apparent impossibility of testing theories with models is due entirely to not going far enough. It will be argued subsequently that if one builds a model of the theory and also builds a model of a conceivable counter-example to the *theory* in question, then, using ordinary test conventions, convincing tests can be performed!

2.2. Testing with models of counter-examples

Prior to discussing the difficulties encountered when performing a convincing test in this way, we need to investigate what constitutes a counter-example and when a model of a counter-example constitutes a refutation of the theory. Rather than building a model of a theory to see whether it 'fits' the available data, considering counter-examples amounts to another approach to testing theories by building models. Before we proceed to build a model by adding what I earlier called 'simplifying assumptions' (i.e. extra assumptions concerning the functional relationship between the endogenous and exogenous variables recognized by the 'behavioural assumptions'), we might try to identify one or more propositions that are directly denied by the behavioural assumptions alone (i.e. without benefit of further specifications).

At first this approach seems too easy. Consider a theory which has several endogenous variables but has only one exogenous variable. Following my discussion in Chapter 6, we could say that any two observations of the values of the endogenous and exogenous variables which show that the values of the exogenous variable did not change, but also show that one or more of the endogenous variables did change, constitutes a refutation of that theory. For endogenous variables to change at least one exogenous variable must change. We can thus say that the observation of changes in endogenous variables without changes in the posited exogenous variables constitutes a counter-example for the theory in question. In the performance of this test we can see that two observations (of all variables) may constitute a refutation.

There are other conceivable counter-examples which may require more. When we consider theories which recognize many exogenous variables, things get much more complex and the minimum number of observations can grow large, as I have shown in Chapters 2 and 3. What constitutes a counter-example is also limited by considerations of quantificational logic. To use the philosopher's example, if our theory is merely that all swans are white, then the observation of just one non-white swan would constitute a counter-example. If our theory were, instead, that there is at least one pink swan, then the observation of a counter-example is impossible. The counter-example in this case amounts to a collection of observations sufficiently large to prove that all swans are non-pink.

Strictly speaking, one does not observe a counter-example directly. Instead, one builds a model of a conceivable counter-example *relevant* for the theory such that verifying the model would necessarily refute the theory. This requirement of relevance is apparently not widely appreciated. It is often violated in discussions of Giffen effects. Would the observation of the Giffen effect logically ever be considered a refutation of traditional ordinal demand theory? At first blush everyone might answer 'yes'. But on logical grounds such a question is very misleading since it would presume that we have a complete theory of the downward-sloping demand curve – i.e. of the so-called Law of Demand. It may have been the intended purpose of demand theory to explain why demand curves are always downward sloping [Hicks 1956, p. 59] but ordinal demand theory never succeeded in doing so [Samuelson 1953, pp. 1-2]. Simply stated, the existence of a Giffen effect is not completely denied by ordinal demand theory, hence its observation cannot be considered a refutation [see Samuelson 1948].[1]

In general terms, whether a particular observation constitutes a test (i.e. a refutation or a verification) of a given theory necessarily depends on what that theory logically affirms or denies. Such dependence (or 'relevance') is never a matter of judgement. It is always a matter of logic. What constitutes a test always depends on what is put at stake within the theory being tested. Whenever a theory is claimed to be true and informative, it must be denying specific observations. The more informative the theory, the more observations denied. This connection between informativeness and the number of conceivable counter-examples is the keystone of

---

1 Alternatively, it can be argued that Giffen effects are contrary to our traditional theory of prices [see Boland 1977d]. Demand theory itself is traditionally offered as logical support for our equilibrium theory of prices. Elsewhere I have gone further to argue that downward-sloping demand curves are necessary for a stable equilibrium in a world of truly independent decision-makers [see Boland 1977b, 1986]. In this sense ordinal demand theory is intended to be a complete set of reasons for why demand curves are downward sloping. And in particular, those reasons are required to be consistent with independent decision-making. As is well known, the traditional demand theory is only able to tell us when Giffen effects will occur (e.g. the implications of the Slutsky relations – a Giffen effect implies a counter income effect that is stronger than the substitution effect of a change in price). Thus, apart from price theory, Giffen effects are not denied and the simple observation of a Giffen effect alone would not constitute a test of ordinal demand theory, no matter what one means by 'testing'. Such testing in this case is simply not relevant.

both Popper's philosophy of science and Samuelson's methodology of searching for 'operationally meaningful propositions'. But more important, it is the significance of what is denied by a theory that determines how much is at stake.

Let us assume away some of our irritants. Let us assume (1) that relevance is not a problem, (2) that we can test theories without having to build models, and (3) that, for the sake of argument, the logical consistency of the set of assumptions constituting the theory or model has not yet been established. Now let us consider a *simultaneous test* of a theory and one of its many counter-examples. On the one hand, in Chapter 2 we recognized that it is impossible to verify a theory by showing that the theory 'fits' one observation of all of its variables – that is, by finding a 'good fit' with the available data – since there is no guarantee that more observations tomorrow will also 'fit'.[2] However, if a counter-example does 'fit' the data (e.g. an observed change in endogenous variables without a change in the exogenous variables) then, so long as we accept the observations as true statements, we would have to admit that any logically complete and consistent theory which denies the counter-example in question has been refuted. That is, in any combination of the theory and this counter-example, both cannot be true.

Consider now the four possible outcomes of a combined simultaneous test of the theory and one of its counter-examples. If neither the theory nor the counter-example fits the available data then we could easily argue that the theory must not be consistent. If both the theory and its counter-example fit the available data then again it is easy to argue that the theory could not be consistent. Of course, these conclusions are based on the acceptance of the observations as true. If the theory is logically consistent then we would expect that any combined simultaneous test of the theory and one of its counter-examples will yield a fit of either the theory or its counter-example – i.e. at least one, but not both. When it is the counter-example that fits, the theory is obviously refuted – either directly because the counter-example is 'verified' or indirectly by saying that even if the theory somehow fits, it would have revealed an inconsistency. When the theory fits but the counter-example does not, then not much has been accomplished. On the one hand, such an event is a minimum condition for logical

---

[2] For example, observing only white swans to date does not assure us that tomorrow we will not see a non-white swan.

consistency. On the other hand, it is still only a single fit and (as I have already noted) there is no guarantee that the theory will fit future observations (or that other possible counter-examples will fit the current data).

What is important about this combined approach to testing is that, if we accept the observations as being true, we can overcome the problem of the Ambiguity of Direct Model Refutation. To see this we need to reconsider the arguments of Chapter 7 where it was noted that showing that a specific model of a theory does not yield a 'good fit' will not (by itself) prove that the theory being modelled is false until one has proven that there does not exist some other model of the theory which does yield a 'good fit'. While a bad fitting model *of the theory* does not constitute a refutation (even though we accept the observations as true) a good fitting model *of the counter-example of the theory* may constitute a refutation when the observations are considered true. To see this let us again assume the behavioural theory is logically consistent so that either the theory is true or its counter-example is true but not both. Again, when we are using the same data, there are four possible outcomes of a combined simultaneous test of the model of the theory itself and a model of one of its counter-examples. Whenever models of the theory and its counter-example both fit the data, we know there is something wrong with the modelling. If they both do not fit then not much has been accomplished since a bad fit of either the theory or the counter-example runs afoul of the Ambiguity of Direct Model Refutation.

Test model of:		
Theory	*Counter-example*	TEST RESULT
good-fit	good-fit	model inconsistency
good-fit	bad-fit	corroboration
bad-fit	good-fit	refutation
bad-fit	bad-fit	ambiguous

Table 1

Whenever the model of the counter-example fits and the model of the theory does not then this is a strong case against the theory, although we cannot be sure there is no modelling problem. Avoidance of a refutation would require at least a critical examination of the modelling methodology. When the model of the theory fits but the model of the counter-example does not then we have a situation which Popper [1965, p. 220] calls a 'corroboration'. Going beyond Popper we can say that a corroboration would occur whenever the combined simultaneous test of a theory and its counter-example runs the risk of yielding a refutation but the behavioural theory manages to survive. A corroboration means that a refutation could have occurred but did not. These four outcomes are summarized in Table 1.

3. Stochasticism and econometric models

Having now argued that convincing refutations are logically possible – at least, in principle – we should see whether my argument is compromised by the consideration of the difficulties involved in the acceptance of observations as true statements. Any refutation of a theory based on a model of a counter-example still requires the acceptance of the truth of the refuting observation or evidence. As one of my early critics noted, 'The quest for truth and validity is indeed a noble venture. However, the economist exists in a stochastic environment' [Smith 1969, p. 81].

3.1. Stochastic models vs stochastic worlds

The problem with 'stochasticism' is that it takes too much for granted. Modern economists are very fond of claiming (like Professor Smith) that the world is a 'stochastic environment'. This concept of the world is, I think, very misleading. Before examining the significance of stochasticism for my argument (namely, that testing is possible when we include tests of counter-examples), I offer a brief theory of stochasticism in modern economics. My purpose is to show that stochasticism involves model building since it requires an explicit modelling assumption which is possibly false, and thus stochasticism should not be taken for granted. Following this, I will use my brief theory to discuss how econometricians deal with stochasticism.

As I stated in Chapter 1, there are two 'worlds': the 'real' world which we observe and the 'ideal' world of the theory or mathematical model which we construct. When we say the theory (or model) is 'true' we mean that the real and the ideal worlds exactly correspond. Many will argue that there are obvious reasons why, even with true theories, the correspondence will not be exact (e.g. errors of measurement, irrational human behaviour, etc.). For these reasons, modern economists build 'stochastic models' which explicitly accommodate the stochastic nature of the correspondence. For example, we can assume that the measurement errors leave the observations in a normal random distribution about the true values of the ideal world. This means that the correspondence itself is the stochastic element of the model.

It should be noted, thus, that it is the model which is stochastic rather than the world or the 'environment'. Any test of a stochastic model is as much a test of the assumed correspondence as it is of the theory itself. Following our discussion in Chapter 1, *one can choose to see the world as being necessarily stochastic only if one assumes beyond question that one's model is true (and fixed) and thus that any variability of the correspondence is due entirely to the unexplainable changes in the real world.* Thus, stochasticism can be seen to put the truth of our theories beyond question.

I think there is always a serious danger of intellectual dishonesty in asserting that the environment is stochastic. We assume that the 'assumptions' of our theory or model are true because we do not know them to be true. Thus there is no reason for any of them to be put beyond question, as stochasticism seems to presume.

3.2. *Econometrics as a study of stochastic models*

Of course, stochasticism itself is put beyond question in the study of econometric models. Econometrics was a research programme founded in the early 1930s to address the obvious need to be able to confront stochastic statistical data with exact models of economic theories. The usual statistical analysis that one would have learned in a typical mathematics department was not always appropriate for the intended research programme. In the early 1940s an entirely different approach was proposed. The idea then was to make the statistical analysis part of economic theory itself [Haavelmo 1941/44, see also Koopmans 1941, Mann and Wald 1943, and Haavelmo 1943]. While there is some danger in seeing this as an endorsement of stochasticism, Haavelmo was quite aware of the limitations of such an approach and was careful to stress that the approach necessitated separating our stochastic models from our exact theories. Moreover, he stressed that his approach required a thorough commitment to stochastic modelling with no hope of returning to the world of exact models [see Haavelmo 1941/44, pp. 55-9].

Few econometricians seem willing to go all the way with Haavelmo and thus still wish to see a possibility of stochastic models being helpful in the assessment of exact theories and models [e.g. Klein 1957]. Nevertheless, many lessons seem to have been learned from Haavelmo's manifesto, the most important of which is to stress the importance of systematically recognizing that if our theories of the interrelationship of economic variables are true then we ought not treat the observation of one variable as independent of the observations of other variables. The question raised is whether and to what extent are the observation errors also interdependent.

The possibility of interdependent observation errors is manifested in the common emphasis on 'stochastic models in which the error elements are associated with separate structural equations rather than with individual economic variables' [Leontief 1948, p. 402]. For example, rather than using an exact (i.e. non-stochastic) equation such as:

$$C = a + b\mathbf{Y}$$

we would explicitly recognize a 'disturbance term', ε, as follows:

$$C = a + b\mathbf{Y} + \varepsilon$$

The disturbance term accounts for errors in the equation as a whole rather than just for errors resulting from observations of $\mathbf{C}$ and $\mathbf{Y}$. Unfortunately, it also introduces or recognizes other ways of accounting for errors. My colleague, Peter Kennedy, itemizes three ways econometricians account for errors represented by the disturbance term: measurement error, specification error, and what he calls 'human indeterminacy' [Kennedy 1979/85, p. 3]. Measurement error is what I call 'observation error'. A specification error is one possible consequence of decisions made by the model builder. While the occurrence of observation errors is external and independent of the model, specification errors are internal and completely dependent on the nature of the constructed model. By impounding specification errors with observation errors into the disturbance term, econometricians make it extremely difficult to discuss the truth status of one's modelling assumptions. The recognition of 'human indeterminacy' is, of course, allowance for those econometricians who believe in stochasticism. Since I am rejecting stochasticism, 'human indeterminacy' is an unacceptable means of accounting for the magnitude of the disturbance term.

If one restricts econometric model building to practical problems then one would have to say, in Friedman's instrumentalist terms [see Boland 1979a], that the truth status of the model is less important than the usefulness of the results of its application. If one restricts econometrics to instrumentalist methodology, then there may be no need to separate internal inaccuracies introduced by specification errors from the external inaccuracies caused by observation errors. However, if the truth status of our economic theories and models does matter, then econometric modelling which does not treat observation and specification errors separately will not obviously be an appropriate tool for analysis. Stated another way, whenever the truth status of our theoretical and modelling assumptions is at issue, *the only acceptable means of accounting for errors is the recognition of external 'measurement errors'*. Moreover, when the truth status of a model matters, specification errors are always unacceptable and always imply a false *model* (but not necessarily a false theory as I noted in Chapter 7).

Nevertheless, the important point to be retained is that, since economic models are primarily concerned with explicit interrelationships between observable variables, whether the errors of observation are interconnected externally may be an important source of information about the data being used. This is obviously an important consideration for some typical macroeconomic data. For example, consider the standard textbook equation:

$$Y = C + I + G.$$

To the extent that observations of C, I and G may be the result of simple income accounting, we can say that whatever is not considered C or G can be accounted for by calling it I. In this elementary case, the observations are by construction interrelated. Assuming we are dealing with models for which such 'identities' have been eliminated, any information we have about errors of observation will not usually imply an interdependence and thus makes it all the more important to treat observational errors separately from specification errors, particularly when we wish to assess the possibility of specification errors.

3.3. *Alternative views of testing with models*

It might be tempting for some readers to confuse what I am calling 'combined simultaneous testing' with so-called 'non-nested hypothesis testing'. This would be a serious error. Models are said to be non-nested when 'they have separate parametric families and one model cannot be obtained from the others as a limiting process' [Pesaran 1974, p. 155]. One reason for avoiding the confusion is that any non-nested models being tested are *models* of competing theories, such that it is *possible* for all to be false [see Kennedy 1979/85, p. 70; MacKinnon 1983, p. 87] and given my arguments in Chapter 7, for nothing to be accomplished. Depending on test procedure, they all can be confirmed, too. In the case of combined simultaneous tests, the essential counter-example is determined solely on the basis of the single behavioural theory in question (i.e. a single list of exogenous and endogenous variables and thus a single parametric family). More important, the counter-example is not just any contrary theory, as in the case of non-nested models, it is a statement whose truth status is denied by the original behavioural theory. Thus, when models of the theory and its counter-example both fail or both fit the data using the same test procedure, at least we have demonstrated a shortcoming in the modelling method or in the logic of the original behavioural theory.

It is equally important to avoid confusing a combined simultaneous test with what is called an 'encompassing test' [see Hendry 1983]. Ideally, an encompassing test would show that one model of a theory is superior to another model of the same theory by showing that the modelling techniques used in the superior model allows for the explanation of (i.e. encompasses) the results obtained by the inferior model. Both models explain the same data but use different modelling assumptions. The reason for avoiding the confusion is simply that a counter-example is not a competing explanation and moreover, the same modelling assumptions are used to model the theory and the counter-example.

Since the same modelling assumptions are used in a combined simultaneous test and the counter-example is not a competing model or theory, the econometric perspective of either encompassing tests or tests of non-nested alternatives is not obviously a relevant basis for considering combined simultaneous testing.[3]

4. Asymmetries in tests based on stochastic models

Now, with stochasticism and the related aspects of econometrics put in their proper places, let me nevertheless accommodate stochastic models in my theory of convincing tests. The central question here is whether the recognition of *stochastic models* undermines my theory of convincing tests or, as I shall argue, actually emphasizes the need for combined simultaneous tests using counter-examples.

The key question that necessitates the recognition of stochastic models is still the acknowledgement that observation statements are seldom exactly true. Recall that my discussion in Sections 1 and 2 *assumed* that observation statements were (exactly) true. Given that assumption, whenever a model of the counter-example was said to fit the available data, we knew that the compound statement, which is formed of the counter-example plus modelling assumptions, was a true statement. Since the truth of the theory would deny the possibility of our ever building a relevant model of a counter-example of that theory which would fit the data, it was concluded that whenever the counter-example did fit, the theory must be false. Now what happens when the determination of a good fit is not exact (due to inaccuracies of the observations used to determine the fit)?

4.1. A simple example

Consider a simple one-equation model which represents the theory that the level of consumption (C) is a *linear* function of the level of national income (Y):

$$C = a + bY$$

The question at issue will be whether the specification of a two-variable linear model represents the true relationship between C and Y. However, for the purposes of this elementary discussion, we will say we know that there are no other relevant variables so that the only issue is the linearity of the model. Let us say we have

---

[3] Nevertheless, many aspects of non-nested hypothesis testing methodology may still apply to the combined simultaneous testing procedure.

made three observations to determine if the linear relationship holds. With two observations we could deduce values for a and b which are the same for both observations – that is, we solve the pair of simultaneous equations (one equation represents one observation):

$$C_1 = a + bY_1$$
$$C_2 = a + bY_2$$

The third observation is used to test the deduced values of a and b. The question is whether the calculated C which equals $(a + bY_3)$ also equals the observed C_3? In Chapters 2 and 3 any difference between the calculated C and the observed C would both constitute a counter-example and be immediately interpreted as a refutation of the model. But that was primarily due to the assumption that observations were always exactly true.

Let us relax this assumption somewhat by saying the observations are not exact but, unlike ordinary econometric modelling, let us also say we have some independent knowledge of the possible observation errors. If we knew the observations could be wrong by no more than 10 percent, then our criterion for interpreting the third observation must accommodate errors of as much as 10 percent. But most important, if we allow for errors in the determination of whether the third observation constitutes a refutation of the linearity of the equation, we will run the risk of incorrectly claiming that the counter-example fits and thus falsely claiming a refutation of the theory. Similarly, we run the risk of incorrectly claiming that the third observation *confirms* the linearity assumption when in reality the relationship is non-linear. What needs to be appreciated when there are errors in observations is that failure to confirm may not constitute a confirmation of a counter-example. With errors in observations, both the theory and its counter-example could fail to be confirmed by the same observations whenever we make allowances for errors. This will depend on how we decide whether we have confirmation.

To illustrate this asymmetry, let us say that we can make two correct observations but all subsequent observations will be subject to errors of as much as (but no more than) 10 percent. For example, if we correctly observe that $C_1 = 10$, $Y_1 = 20$, $C_2 = 12$ and $Y_2 = 30$, then by assuming linearity we can deduce that $a = 6$ and $b = 0.2$. Now let us say that at the time of our third observation the (unknown) true value of Y_3 is 40 but our third observation is inaccurate, so that we observe $Y_3 = 44$. At the same time, we also observe that $C_3 = 12.6$. Both observed variables are off by about 10 percent. If the true relationship is linear then the true value for C_3 is 14 – but if the true relationship is non-linear, then the true value of C_3 could differ from 14. Assuming linearity is true, our calculated C will be 14.8 which differs from the *observed* C by more than 17 percent, even though neither observation is more than 10 percent wrong. Depending on how we choose to interpret this, we might incorrectly conclude that C and Y are not linearly related when in reality they are.

For the sake of discussion, let us say we doubt that *both* observations would be off by as much as 10 percent so we will interpret a 17 percent calculated difference as a 'bad fit' with regard to our linearity assumption. However, a bad fit in this case does not mean that we have proven that the true model is non-linear. All that we have concluded is that the linearity assumption is not confirmed. For us to conclude that the linearity assumption is false we have to decide what would constitute a counter-example as well as a good fit for a counter-example.

4.2. Disconfirming vs non-confirming observations

In my example I said that it is known that observations could differ from the true values of C and Y by as much as 10 percent and thus when making our third observation, the calculated and observed values of C could be found to differ by as much as 17 percent without necessarily proving that the true relationship is non-linear. By recognizing that non-confirmations of linearity are not necessarily confirmations of non-linearity, it is always possible when adopting conservative test criteria based on single observations that both the theory (linearity) and the counter-example (non-linearity) will fail to be confirmed. Thus a test based on a single observation is not usually considered a very convincing test. This is so even though a single observation of, say, a 20 percent calculated difference in our simple example would constitute a refutation while a zero error does not constitute a proof that the relationship is linear, since the next observation might not be errorless.

Anything short of the maximum possible error in the calculated difference leaves the results of the test doubtful. Nevertheless, we may wish to interpret the test based on any notions we might have about the acceptability of errors. Specifically, we might think that a claim that linearity is confirmed based on a 17 percent allowable error is too risky. Even a 15 percent error might be considered too risky for a confirmation of linearity. We might take the position that while a 15 percent error does not constitute a proof that the model is not linear, such an observation casts serious doubt on the model's linearity. Let us call this interpretation (of the observation) a 'disconfirmation' of the linear model. Similarly, an error of 5 percent may be too risky for a conclusion that the counter-example is confirmed and thereby that the assumption of linearity is definitely false. In this case, the observation may be interpreted as a disconfirmation of the counter-example.

It is important here not to confuse the disconfirmation of a theory with the confirmation of its counter-example. Equally important, we ought not confuse 'not disconfirmed' with a 'confirmation'. While a calculated difference greater than 18 percent may constitute a proof of non-linearity when we know the observations cannot be more than 10 percent wrong, using 18 percent as a test criteria seems too severe. So we need to choose a convenient standard to interpret the calculated difference.

On the one hand, if we are looking for a confirmation of the counter-example, we may wish to say that a calculated error of 15 percent is sufficient for us to conclude that the linearity assumption is false but an error of less than 10 percent is not sufficient, and thus the counter-example is not-confirmed. If we are looking for a disconfirmation of the counter-example, we might say an error of less than 5 percent leads to the conclusion that the counter-example is disconfirmed but an error over 10 percent leads us to declare the counter-example to be not-disconfirmed. On the other hand, a similar disparity can be created when we are directly assessing the linearity assumption. If we are looking for a confirmation of the linearity assumption, we may wish to say that a calculated error of less than 2 percent is sufficient for us to conclude that the linearity assumption is confirmed but an error of more than 10 percent is not sufficient, so that the linearity assumption is not-confirmed. If we are looking for a disconfirmation of the linearity assumption, we might say an error of more than 15 percent leads us to conclude that the linearity assumption is disconfirmed but an error between 5 and 10 percent leads us to declare the linearity assumption to be not-disconfirmed.

Here, of course, I am arbitrarily assigning numbers to the allowable or required criteria for the purposes of discussion. Any actual criteria will be decided on the basis of what we know about the nature of the observation errors and the nature of the actual theory being tested. As my simple example illustrates, it is easy to adopt very different criteria of rejection or of acceptance. I am using the words 'confirmed' and 'disconfirmed' rather than 'true' and 'false' to bring out the essential asymmetry. In the true-false case, 'not-true' means false and 'not-false' means true (so long as we do not deny the axiom of the excluded middle [see Boland 1979a, 1982]). Here, it should be clear that 'not-confirmed' does not necessarily mean disconfirmed and 'not-disconfirmed' does not mean confirmed whenever there is a wide range of possible errors.

In terms familiar to those who have read any elementary statistics book, we have to decide which is more important: avoiding the rejection of a true assumption or avoiding the acceptance of a false assumption. Statisticians refer to these as Type I and Type II errors. What criterion is used to define Type I or Type II errors is still a matter of judgement with a heavy element of arbitrariness. Selecting a criterion which makes it easier to avoid one type of error will usually make it easier to incur the other type of error. Furthermore, whether we use a criterion of 5 percent or 10 percent as allowable deviation in calculated values may be determined more by the economics of the situation than by one's philosophy of science. The cost of making one type of error based on a narrow range of 5 percent may be greater than the other type of error based on a range of 10 percent. When dealing with matters of social policy it may be considered safer to have low standards of accepting a false linearity assumption and high standards for rejecting a true linearity assumption. Since there is usually ample room for doubt, linear models are often easier to apply to practical problems. It all depends on what we are looking for or are willing to accept.

My distinction between disconfirmations and non-confirmations (or maybe even between confirmations and disconfirmations) may not be clear to those familiar only with the concept of hypothesis testing found in statistics textbooks. Once one has chosen to avoid, say, Type I error, then any failure to confirm the counter-example is automatically interpreted as a confirmation of the theory. Furthermore, exclusive concern for Type I error leads to the exclusive use of confirmation criteria. Concern for Type II error would have us use disconfirmation criteria instead. If for any reason we are unwilling to choose between Type I and Type II error, then we will need to be able to distinguish between disconfirmations and non-confirmations.

4.3. Confirmation vs disconfirmation test criteria

The possible asymmetry between confirmation and disconfirmation criteria needs to be seen against the background of the problems I have already discussed concerning the process of testing theories using models of those theories. Even when we considered observations to be without errors, we still could not expect to be able to refute a theory by refuting just one singular model of that theory. However, I did show in Section 2.2 that if we simultaneously test a model of a theory and a model of its counter-example, it is possible to say what would constitute a refutation of a theory. Specifically, a refutation would occur when the model of the theory fails to fit the data while the model of a counter-example does fit. Now, what is added to this by entertaining the possibility of observational errors?

If we were to base our combined simultaneous test on a single observation of the theory and a coincident observation of its counter-example, we would be wise to adopt rather conservative criteria of acceptance or rejection – maybe, as in my simple example, something like 2 percent for confirming observations of linearity vs 15 percent for a confirmation of an observation of the counter-example. The difficulty here is that a single observation test is one-dimensional. It is necessary then to distinguish between a 'confirming observation' and a 'confirmation' which may require many confirming observations. Similarly, a 'disconfirming observation' is distinguished from a 'disconfirmation' which may require many disconfirming observations.

Since observation errors are possible and we might not wish to jump to a conclusion on a single observation, let us now repeat the third observation (of **C** and **Y**) 19 more times. This new dimension (the number of observations) raises a new question for decision: how many non-confirming observations will we allow in a confirmation? No more than 1 in 20? Maybe 2 in 20? Given that observation errors are possible, let us consider alternative postures concerning how to interpret the results of 20 observations.[4] Our test criteria and our posture must, of course, be decided before

---

4 Note that requiring a minimum of 20 stochastic observations to play the same role of one non-stochastic observation means that a stochastic version of a non-stochastic model (such as one from Chapter 3) which has a P-dimension of, say, 30 would now have an effective P-dimension of 600. This means a model for which it would have taken at least a year to construct a refutation would now require at least 20 years to refute!

making the observations if we wish to avoid unnecessary skepticism. The following represent four different and illustrative postures that employ only confirmation/non-confirmation criteria for the assessment of observations:

(1) We might say that whenever 5 or more of the 20 observations are convincing *confirming observations* of linearity (no more than 2 percent calculated difference, as discussed in Section 4.1) we will conclude that the linear model is *confirmed*, otherwise it is *not confirmed*.

(2) We might say that whenever 5 or more of the 20 observations are convincing *confirming observations* of non-linearity (at least 15 percent calculated difference) we will conclude that a model of a counter-example of the linear model is *confirmed*, otherwise it is *not confirmed*.

(3) We might say that whenever 5 or more of the 20 observations are not convincing *confirming observations* of linearity (more than 2 percent calculated difference) we will conclude that the linear model is *disconfirmed*, otherwise it is *not disconfirmed*.

(4) We might say that whenever 5 or more of the 20 observations are not convincing *confirming observations* of non-linearity (less than 15 percent calculated difference) we will conclude that a counter-example of the linear model is *disconfirmed*, otherwise it is *not disconfirmed*.

Given that our criteria for convincing observations might be considered extreme (2 percent or less in one case and at least 15 in the other), it may be reasonable not to expect a large proportion of observations to be meeting either criterion. Thus, we have an asymmetry between the confirmation of a counter-example and a disconfirmation of the theory itself. Even though we have employed a confirmation/non-confirmation criterion (to assess observations), in order to define the four interpretation postures we still need to decide whether we are more interested in finding disconfirmations or confirmations – although there may not be any non-arbitrary way to do so.

Let me illustrate the possible consequences of all this for combined simultaneous tests of the model of a theory and a model of its counter-example. If we recognize that 'not-confirmed' does not imply disconfirmed, then to illustrate the possible outcome, depending on whether we are looking for confirmations or discon-firmations as defined in statements (1) to (4) above, we need two tables. In Table 2, the presumption is that the socially acceptable testing conventions only identify a confirmation, as in the case of desiring to avoid Type I errors. And in Table 3 it is presumed that only disconfirmations are identified (avoiding Type II errors).

Confirmation-based test model of:		
Theory	*Counter-example*	TEST RESULT
confirmed	confirmed	inconclusive
confirmed	not-confirmed	weak conditional corroboration
not-confirmed	confirmed	conditional refutation
not-confirmed	not-confirmed	inconclusive

Table 2

Disconfirmation-based test model of:		
Theory	*Counter-example*	TEST RESULT
not-disconfirmed	not-disconfirmed	inconclusive
not-disconfirmed	disconfirmed	conditional corroboration
disconfirmed	not-disconfirmed	weak conditional refutation
disconfirmed	disconfirmed	inconclusive

Table 3

In Tables 2 and 3, I have noted that all corroborations or refutations must be considered conditional. The condition is that the interpretation of the result is always dependent on the acceptance of the specified test criteria used. In the case of my simple example above, the criteria involve the possibly extreme limit of a 2 percent acceptable error between the calculated and observed C. Other criteria are possible such as limiting the ratio of acceptable to unacceptable errors in the given number of observations made. In both tables the inconclusive results may cause one to question the test criteria in a single equation model. In multiple equation models inconclusive results might also suggest that the model could be either incomplete or inconsistent.

As long as one is willing (a) to not demand unconditional refutations, (b) to adopt standard views of testing and thus commit oneself to which type of error (I or II) to avoid, and (c) to commit oneself to use either a confirmation or a disconfirmation criterion for the evaluation of observations, then I think by making all tests of a theory combined simultaneous tests of the model of the theory and of at least one counter-example to the theory, refutations in economics are in principle possible, albeit conditional.[5]

4.4. The irrelevance of the probability approach

So far, I have not said anything about probabilities. Many readers will find this irritating because they think probabilities are essential for a discussion of conclusions drawn from inaccurate observations, that is, from stochastic models. While the probability approach to economics [e.g. Haavelmo 1941/44] may appear to solve some of these problems, it too often masks from view the logical structure that defines the methodological problem at hand. If we wish to discuss things in probability terms then, instead of saying that errors of observation could be as much as 10 percent, we could *assume* that when we repeatedly make the third observation, the possible errors for this observation will be distributed in a manner we associate with the Gaussian 'normal distribution' (i.e. the bell-shaped curve). If we also assume that the average value of the observation is the true observation, then the formal mathe-

---

5 Some of my students have made elementary applications of this approach to testing in economics. What is most striking from their applications, where they have repeated previously reported tests of mainstream economic theories, is that in almost every case the reported results do not correspond to the decisive categories but to the inconclusive results. For another explanation of this approach to testing and how it can be used, see Bennett [1981]; Jensen, Kamath and Bennett [1987].

matical properties of such a curve can be used to calculate the probability that the observations will be incorrect in more than, say, 5 percent of the observations. In doing so, we facilitate a calculation of potential damage done by incorrectly accepting a fit. If we have no reason to assume that errors are normally distributed or if we know something about the observation process independent of both the model and the testing process, then some probability presumptions may be a major source of difficulty. I suspect that the primary reason for promoting probabilistic approaches to economics is that they provide a basis for formalizing the arbitrary decisions regarding the choice of confirmation or disconfirmation criteria. Some people simply feel better when necessary arbitrariness is formalized.

Nevertheless, for some practical problems where the assessment of benefits and costs are unproblematic (and there is no independent means of assessing the accuracy of observations), characterizing the occurrence of errors to be governed by a given probability distribution can be very helpful. But if we do not know how the errors are distributed, more questions may be begged than are answered [cf. Swamy, Conway, and von zur Muehlen 1985]. I think for the purposes of understanding the difficulties in forming conclusions when there are errors in observations, it is better not to confuse stochastic models with probabilistic models. As I have attempted to show in this section, the problems and means of avoiding the Ambiguity of Direct Model Refutation *do not require* a probabilistic approach to testing stochastic models.

5. 'Normative' vs 'positive' methodology

While the many critics of Popper's philosophy of science or of Samuelson's methodology may have been encouraged by Chapter 7 and its pessimistic look at the possibility of refuting a theory, it is unlikely that those critics will be very pleased with my conclusion that refutations are possible whenever we agree on the testing conventions and test both the model of the theory and a model of its counter-example. My purpose here is not, however, to defend Popper or Samuelson but merely to represent what I think is a viable interpretation of what is possible, given what ordinary economic model builders seem willing to accept in terms of testing conventions or criteria.

Perhaps, as the critics charge, mainstream economists ought to be attempting to refute neoclassical economic theory. However, on the basis of Chapter 7 we can certainly understand why economists would not waste their time attempting to build models of an economic theory merely to refute it. Economists ought not to be scolded for not doing impossible tasks. Many model builders in economics will see themselves, nevertheless, engaged in an ongoing programme of inventing and refuting an endless series of specific models. It is important for methodologists, who claim to be explaining what mainstream economists are actually doing, to attempt to construct a view of testing that corresponds to what is actually practiced. In this chapter I have presented such a view of testing in economics, but I have not stopped there. I have offered a view of testing that overcomes the obstacles to direct tests of economic theories without requiring any substantial changes in the socially accepted testing conventions currently used by practicing model builders in economics.

EPILOGUE

Methodology after Samuelson:
Lessons for Methodologists

Foundations of Economic Analysis had successes in
generating a wide variety of substantive theories. But
what interested its young author most ... was the success
it could achieve in formulating a general theory of
economic theories.

Paul A. Samuelson [1983, p. xxvii]

a good deal of [the Conference's] time was devoted to
methodological discussions; Professor Popper cast a long
shadow over our proceedings! This was regrettable since
most of the papers had something to teach us while the
methodological arguments had not. We had all been
through them since undergraduate days ... these things are
as much a matter of temperament and what one likes
doing as they are of philosophy of which most of us are
pretty ignorant. I simply record that, in my view, the
Conference would have been better than it was if we had
spent more time on what people were saying in their
papers than on what they ought to have been saying.

Frank H. Hahn [1965a, p. xi]

In this closing chapter I wish to share with methodologists some of
the lessons I have learned from a research programme in applied
methodology that has spanned more than twenty years. What I
have learned from my specific research programme (concerning
how apparently innocuous modelling assumptions and techniques
can affect the testability of one's model) should be evident in the
previous eight chapters. So, in this chapter I wish to discuss what I
learned about the methodology of economics in general with
special emphasis given to Samuelson's impact on the field of
economic methodology.

Often I have taken the opportunity to point out that Paul Samuelson's book, **Foundations of Economic Analysis**, was intentionally a methodology book. Here I wish also to point out that it represented very good methodology, despite its being an operationalist version of what is often alleged to be Karl Popper's falsificationist methodology.

Unlike many of today's methodologists, Professor Samuelson did more than just talk about his methodology. Like the good methodologist that he is, Samuelson proceeded to show how to implement his methodology. In this sense, I think we can all agree that Samuelson has been a most successful methodologist. Here I shall examine the consequences of Samuelson's impressive success as a practicing methodologist for the profession of economic methodologists.

Samuelson repeatedly noted that his book demonstrates how the development of economic theory is intimately intertwined with successful efforts to meet one methodological goal – namely, theories progress by creating 'operationally meaningful propositions'. Explaining the development of economic theory is always an intellectual juggling act. There are two balls to juggle – one's theory of economic phenomena and one's theory of economic theories. Theorists as methodologists are always trying to keep these two balls in the air. And as with all juggling acts, if we concentrate on just one ball, the other ball will usually come crashing down.

Now, I wish to extend this two-ball approach to recognize explicitly that methodology as a 'general theory of economic theories' always involves both rhetoric and the sociology of science. It involves both because they are both necessary and because rhetoric and sociology should not be considered separately. Rather than a mere two-ball juggling act, we will need to consider a four-ball juggling approach to economic methodology. Again, the important point to keep in mind is that whenever we concentrate on one ball at the expense of the others, the other balls will surely be dropped.

1. The interdependence of sociology and rhetoric

There are some methodologists today who argue that we should concentrate exclusively on rhetoric of economics (e.g. Arjo Klamer and followers of Donald McCloskey) while others argue that we should concentrate on the sociology of economics (e.g. Bob Coats).

I think both of these arguments are misleading from the perspective of methodology since sociology and rhetoric are interdependent. Moreover, both are implicitly dealt with in any methodological study. Before analyzing the juggling skills of any good methodologist, let me examine what I think is the necessary interdependence of sociology and rhetoric.

The well-known Canadian communications theorist, Marshall McLuhan, is famous for pointing out that *how* we say something is usually more informative than *what* we say. I think this is true for both economic methodology and economic methodologists. To understand McLuhan's observation and its relevance for economic methodology, I wish to consider the following question: How can the method of presentation by itself ever be informative? The answer which I wish to defend here is as follows: The message of one's statement or argument is dictated to a great extent by the medium of its presentation.

1.1. The medium IS the message

The effectiveness of any method of presenting a statement depends profoundly on the nature of the audience to whom the statement is directed. Some methods are better than others. If the audience is a convention of religious fundamentalists, quoting from the approved scripture will be essential. If the audience is a meeting of mathematical economists, one must put statements in the form of 'propositions', 'lemmas' and the other paraphernalia of mathematical formalism. If the audience is a gathering of ...

Well, I think you get the idea. What you say will be considered 'informative' only when it is properly stated. What is proper is not a matter for free choice since it is dictated by the tastes of the intended audience.

Rhetoric is the study of what it actually takes to convince a given audience. That is, rhetoric is concerned with the requirements of 'effectiveness'. If every audience were made up of independently thinking individuals – ones like those studied by neoclassical economists – then perhaps rhetoric would be a simple matter of psychology [see Boland 1982]. Unfortunately, only one out of twenty people are independent thinkers [Wilson 1963, p. 318]. This is not a matter of psychology but a recognition that our educational system does not promote independent thinking. When I say that most people are not independent thinkers, I am merely saying that what most people think depends on what other people think. Such an interdependence is directly a matter of sociology since whenever one studies rhetoric, one is implicitly (if not explicitly) studying sociology.

Sociology is, among other things, a study of the basis for interdependent decision-making. That is, it studies how one individual's decisions depend on expectations of what other people will do and expect [see Boland 1979b]. Social institutions and conventions provide a convenient basis for forming such expectations. When approaching an audience of economists, for example, we take for granted that they know the contents of a standard principles textbook and thus expect them to know what a demand curve is. A more obvious example is the requirement that one must understand the language which the audience speaks if one ever hopes to get a point across. But rhetoric is more than a matter of language. Successful rhetoric involves using the conventional 'truths' to build convincing arguments. Institutions and published norms of social behaviour are important sources of the information needed to make everyday decisions. Interdependence of decision-makers at some level must involve the method of how one decision-maker is convinced by the actions or arguments of another decision-maker. Thus the study of sociology always involves the study of rhetoric. Despite what some neoclassical economists want us to believe, information that is only about prices is never enough – but I will leave this digression for a future study.

1.2. Methodology as a juggling act

Recall that Samuelson, the methodologist, said that he wished to be successful 'in formulating a general theory of economic theories' – that is, in explaining what economic theorists do. What I have been saying is that to be successful, a methodologist must be a skillful juggler. The methodologist not only must (1) understand the logic of explanation, but must (2) understand economic theory, (3) understand what the audience for that explanation knows or takes for granted, and (4) know what it would take to convince that audience. This is no easy juggling act because these four requirements must be met in a logically consistent manner. Moreover, any methodologist who tries to deal with these requirements by keeping them separate – perhaps to reap the benefits of a division of labour – is not likely to be successful or appreciated by anyone.

Let us consider the application of a division of labour to methodology. Contrary to what we teach in our principles courses, a division of labour does not always lead to an optimum. Nevertheless, it is too tempting to think that each of the essential elements of methodology would benefit from the expertise of specialists. For example, it is quite common for methodologists today to consult a philosophy of science textbook to obtain a solid foundation for an understanding of the logic of explanation. Unfortunately, this approach to understanding falsely presumes a solid unanimity among philosophers of science. Even so, some young economic methodologists think that a spectacular demonstration of an understanding of one particular philosophy of science is all that it takes to be a methodologist. Let us leave aside the question of how boring it would be for a juggler to juggle just one object. For us the question is, who is the audience for such a demonstration? This is an important question since, as I said above, the sociology and rhetoric of that audience will dictate the appropriate method and substance for one's demonstration.

Samuelson may not be immune from this criticism of misplaced specialization. Samuelson seems to suggest that he was merely implementing an 'operationalist' methodology, namely the one which says that an acceptable explanation of a phenomenon requires us to specify how to measure it. If Samuelson really was implementing such a philosophically prescribed methodology, as he seemed to suggest, then Joan Robinson's criticism challenging a unique measure of capital would have destroyed Samuelson's version of economics. But her critique failed to convince everyone simply because Samuelson was going beyond the philosophers of science rather than blindly following them. More important, the audience to which Samuelson directed his **Foundations of Economic Analysis** did not understand the philosophy of operationalism sufficiently to comprehend the substance of the debate and thus were unable to appreciate his methodology or the logic of Mrs Robinson's critique. Unfortunately, his audience still is convinced more by form than substance and continue to think he won but they seem unable to explain why.

2. History and reality

I would like to continue to illustrate the pitfalls of relying on specialists in such other things as rhetoric, sociology or mathematics but I must move along. The time has come for me to attempt to practice what I am preaching in this closing chapter, so, I turn to the sociology of the economics profession with an eye on its rhetoric, paying particular attention to the role of methodology and the methodologist. We need to examine the evolution of the sociology of our profession because it contributed more to Samuelson's success as a methodologist than did the veracity of his particular opinions about methodology.

To begin let me acknowledge what I think is the dominant empirical feature of the sociology of our profession since about 1960. Most mainstream economists are convinced that methodological discussions are a waste of time [e.g. see Hahn 1965a]. Of course, mainstream economists are probably right but let us suspend our judgement and first try to understand this reality. The key word is 'mainstream' and the question is: Why is methodology no longer a part of the profession's mainstream? I think this is an important question and, to illustrate, let me ask a couple more.

The first question is: How many 'top ten' North American universities' economics programmes are represented at the typical History of Economics Society meetings (the only conference in North America where methodology is openly and regularly discussed)? To answer this question I consulted the official list of participants for the 1986 meetings of this august society. I could not find even one person from Harvard, Stanford, MIT, UCLA, Yale, Princeton, Pennsylvania, Berkeley or Chicago. And just to add some perspective to this question, I looked up each member of MIT's faculty to see where they obtained their PhDs and of the thirty-four listed in the **American Economic Association Handbook**, ten were from Harvard, nine from MIT, and one or two from each of Princeton, Chicago, Pennsylvania and Yale. The only school represented in both lists is Columbia which is understandable since that was the location of the 1986 History of Economics Society meetings. For all practical purposes one can conclude that there is nothing in common between the interests of the members of the History of Economics Society who promote the study of economic methodology and the professors in the mainstream of the economics profession.

The second question is: How many methodology papers were published in the top economics journals between 1967, the publication year for the last major contribution [i.e. Bear and Orr 1967] to the methodological discussion initiated by Samuelson's famous critique of Friedman's methodology, and 1979, the year that I, with the help of Mark Perlman, stirred up the same hornet's nest with my infamous **Journal of Economic Literature** article? If by 'top journals' we mean the **American Economic Review** or the

Journal of Political Economy, then the answer is *two* articles. The only articles that stand out from that period are the 1971 **Journal of Political Economy** article by Louis De Alessi and the 1973 **American Economic Review** article by Stanley Wong. The important point here is that for twelve years methodology was virtually banned from the pages of the leading journals. There was a brief period of about five years when Robert Clower allowed methodologists some limited access to the **American Economic Review**, but unfortunately the door seems to be closed again.

So, the sociological facts of our economics profession are that, with the possible exception of Samuelson, there are no methodologists in the top mainstream economics departments and with the exception of a brief moment in the sun during the early 1980s, there has been virtually no methodology in the leading journals since Samuelson's final word on 'theory and realism' [Samuelson 1965]. I claim that if one wishes to be successful as a professional methodologist today, then one must somehow understand and overcome these sociological facts.

2.1. Understanding the sociology of the economics profession

Since we are all products of the profession we wish to study, we should be able to draw upon our own experiences. My graduate education, or should I say training, in economics was exclusively in mathematical economics. This was inevitable since I came to economics from an undergraduate programme in mechanical engineering. I point this out because it is just this type of educational programming that systematically rules out any consideration of the philosophical questions inherent in the study of methodology. When I announced to my undergraduate teachers that I wished to study methodology they patiently explained to me the error of my ways. So off I went to study mathematical economics since I supposedly had the requisite engineering mentality to do so.

As we all know, what was once just a special area in economics has since grown to dominate all of economics. Today, virtually all graduates of the leading mainstream schools are well-trained economics engineers. Their teachers send them off into the world to seek out 'operationally meaningful' (i.e. refutable) economics propositions. This normative prescription is their only concession to doing something other than strict applied economics. What should be apparent here is that mainstream economics today is the reification and embodiment of nothing other than Samuelson's

Foundations. The pre-eminent problem facing someone who wishes to study methodology is not that methodology has been banned from the workplace but rather that there is only one methodology. Methodology is no longer an interesting research topic for the mainstream simply because the choice has been made and there is nothing more to argue.

Why has Samuelson's methodology been so successful in dominating the mainstream profession's methodological choices? Of course, this will have to be answered by some sort of revealed preference analysis. I think the overwhelming aspect of Samuelson's **Foundations** and its embodied methodology is his implicit rejection of any need to appeal to the authority of philosophers. I applaud his anti-authoritarianism. However, cynics might wish to point out that he rejects philosophy only because he wished us to appeal to the authority of mathematicians, but let us leave that touchy issue aside for now. If we keep our eyes wide open, I think it is easy to see that the methodological motto over the door of every mainstream economics department is:

WHEN IT COMES TO METHODOLOGY, TALK IS CHEAP,
SO LET YOUR ACTIONS DO THE TALKING.

In small print just under this motto is the additional normative proscription: PHILOSOPHERS SHOULD MIND THEIR OWN BUSINESS.

2.2. *Overcoming the sociology of the profession*

Clearly, if I am correct about why Samuelson's methodology is so dominating, would-be methodologists will have to avoid invoking the authority of philosophers if they want the study of methodology to be respected and accepted in the mainstream. By this statement, I am not trying to suggest that the mainstream has made a correct methodological choice – I am only trying to be realistic about what it takes to be successful in the mainstream of economics.

An obvious alternative to my suggestion is for methodologists to group together into a special-interest group or subdiscipline much as the mathematical economists did in the 1930s. Perhaps we can convince one of the leading journals to devote part of their journal space to us or maybe we can even have our own journal. This way, it might be argued, methodologists can get their papers published and thus they can get tenure like the mainstream economists do. While this surely is a more enjoyable way to spend one's time as a methodologist than continually banging one's head on the doors of mainstream departments, I am still not optimistic about its possibility of success. There are two reasons for this. One concerns the question of the inappropriateness of the division of labour which I have already discussed. The other reason concerns the obvious need to demonstrate standards of scholarship that invite respect.

Those methodologists who promote methodology as a separate subdiscipline run the risk of suggesting that one can successfully study methodology as a topic separate from the rest of economics. The worst of this danger is the temptation to invoke the perceived standards of the philosophy profession. There is no reason in the world to think that a philosopher is a better judge of what is appropriate to convince an audience of economists than the economists themselves. As I have been arguing, the audience matters most. Besides, some of the concerns of philosophers are silly by anyone's standards. But most important, if we surrender to the temptation to use ready-made arguments from philosophy books, we turn away from the lesson to be learned from Samuelson's success. One of the major reasons why Samuelson's methodology was so successful is that he openly rejected the usual type of methodology [see Metzler 1948]. Actually, what he rejected was professional philosophy and its authoritarian and prescriptive tendencies.

3. Lessons for would-be methodologists

Many of us think that the methodological issues embodied in neo-classical economic theory are not dead issues and are still worthy of further discussion and criticism. The key question is: How are professional methodologists ever going to survive and prosper when so many mainstream economists think methodological discussion is a waste of time? I have been arguing that to answer this question we need to study the history of Samuelson's success as a methodologist rather than promote philosophers such as Popper. Moreover, the lessons we learn from Samuelson's success we must never violate. Let me now summarize the lessons I think I have learned.

Lesson 1: Hahn is typical

The opinions of Frank Hahn, quoted at the beginning of this chapter, are typical of mainstream economics. While it might be possible at the department of economics of Podunk University to find a receptive audience which will delight in hearing a paper offering a spirited rendition of the maxims of your favourite philosopher of science, hardly any mainstream economist will read anything more than its title. No matter how well your paper is written, no major journal will waste its time or funds having it reviewed.

Lesson 2: Cookbook methodology is unappetizing

Mainstream economists react very negatively to papers which offer cookbook recipes for 'proper' and 'improper' scientific methods. Such papers turn the average economist off because they involve preaching to economists that they must view economic methodology in accordance with the author's favourite philosopher of science. In my student days Karl Popper was the object of worship. Today the fad is Imre Lakatos. Maybe tomorrow it will be Ian Hacking. It will not matter who the current hero or heroine is, mainstream economists will not be interested.

Lesson 3: Methodology does not always matter

What these negative lessons tell us is that we cannot presume that there is an automatic audience for philosophy of economics or for any bag of methodological judgements. What can we conclude that might have some positive flavour? From the history of Samuelson's success I think we can conclude that actions speak louder than words. Rather than extolling the virtues of rhetorical methods or literary criticism, demonstrate how the mainstream economist can learn from such methodology. Rather than extolling the virtues of sociological analysis, demonstrate how the mainstream economist can benefit from such analysis. Rather than extolling the virtues of the philosophy of science of Hacking or Lakatos, demonstrate for the mainstream economists why such a discussion will ever matter.

Samuelson's success was made possible by his ability to demonstrate how his view of methodology matters in the development of economic theory. What impressed his audience was not his dazzling display of philosophical cleverness, but rather the demonstration of his thorough understanding of economic theory. His success amounts to an outstanding juggling act. He demonstrated how his view of methodology is inseparable from his understanding of economic theory. And, as I have claimed, his success depended on his clear understanding of both the sociology of the economics profession and its rhetoric. I think the audience was very impressed with his skillful juggling act. Moreover, their preferences have been clearly revealed for all would-be methodologists to see.

Bibliography

Abramovitz, M. (ed.) [1959] **Allocation of Economic Resources** (Stanford: Stanford University Press)

Agassi, J. [1959] 'Corroboration versus induction' **British Journal for the Philosophy of Science, 36**, 311-17

Agassi, J. [1961] 'The role of corroboration in Popper's methodology' **Australian Journal of Philosophy, 34**, 82-91

Agassi, J. [1963] **Towards an Historiography of Science, History and Theory, Beiheft 2** (The Hague: Mouton)

Agassi, J. [1966a] 'Sensationalism' **Mind, 75**, 1-24

Agassi, J. [1966b] 'The confusion between science and technology in the standard philosophies of science' **Technology and Culture, 7**, 348-66

Agassi, J. [1967] 'Planning for success: a reply to Professor Wisdom' **Technology and Culture, 8**, 78-81

Agassi, J. [1971a] 'Tautology and testability in economics' **Philosophy of Social Science, 1**, 49-63

Agassi, J. [1971b] 'Tristram Shandy, Pierre Menard, and all that' **Inquiry, 14**, 152-81

Alchian, A. and W. Allen [1967] **University Economics** (Belmont: Wadsworth)

Allen, W. [1977] 'Economics, economists, and economic policy: modern American experiences' **History of Political Economy, 9**, 48-88

Archibald, G.C. [1960] 'Testing marginal productivity theory' **Review of Economic Studies, 27**, 210-13

Archibald, G.C. [1961] 'Chamberlin versus Chicago' **Review of Economic Studies, 29**, 1-28

Archibald, G.C. [1966] 'Refutation or comparison' **British Journal for the Philosophy of Science, 17**, 279-96

Arrow, K. [1951/63] **Social Choice and Individual Values** (New York: Wiley)

Arrow, K. [1959] 'Towards a theory of price adjustment' in Abramovitz [1959], 41-51

Arrow, K. [1968] 'Mathematical models in the social sciences' in Brodbeck [1968], 635-67

Arrow, K. and G. Debreu [1954] 'Existence of an equilibrium for a competitive economy' **Econometrica, 22**, 265-90

Arrow, K. and F. Hahn [1971] **General Competitive Analysis** (San Francisco: Holden-Day)

Bartley, W.W. [1964a] **The Retreat to Commitment** (London: Chatto & Windus)

Bartley, W.W. [1964b] 'Rationality vs the Theory of Rationality' in Bunge [1964], 3-31

Bartley, W.W. [1968] 'Theories of demarcation between science and metaphysics' in Lakatos and Musgrave [1968], 40-64

Bator, F.M. [1957] 'The simple analytics of welfare maximization' **American Economic Review, 47**, 22-59

Bear, D. and D. Orr [1967] 'Logic and expediency in economic theorizing' **Journal of Political Economy, 75**, 188-96

Bell, R. [1912] **A Treatise on the Coordinate Geometry of Three Dimensions** (London: Macmillan)

Bennett, R. [1981] **An Empirical Test of some Post-Keynesian Income Distribution Theories**, PhD thesis, Simon Fraser University, Burnaby, B.C.

Blanché, R. [1965] **Axiomatics** (New York: The Free Press of Glencoe)

Blaug, M. [1968] **Economic Theory in Retrospect** 2nd edn (Homewood: Irwin)

Blaug, M. [1978] **Economic Theory in Retrospect** 3rd edn (Cambridge: Cambridge University Press)

Blaug, M. [1980] **The Methodology of Economics** (Cambridge: Cambridge University Press)

Bohm, P. [1967] 'On the theory of "second best"' **Review of Economic Studies, 34**, 81

Boland, L. [1966] **On the Methodology of Economic Model Building**, PhD thesis, University of Illinois, Urbana, Ill.

Boland, L. [1968] 'The identification problem and the validity of economic models' **South African Journal of Economics, 36**, 236-40

Boland, L. [1969] 'Economic understanding and understanding economics' **South African Journal of Economics, 37**, 144-60

Boland, L. [1970a] 'Conventionalism and economic theory' **Philosophy of Science, 37**, 239-48

Boland, L. [1970b] 'Axiomatic analysis and economic understanding' **Australian Economic Papers, 9**, 62-75

Boland, L. [1971] 'Methodology as an exercise in economic analysis' **Philosophy of Science, 38**, 105-17

Boland, L. [1974] 'Lexicographic orderings, multiple criteria, and "ad hocery"' **Australian Economic Papers, 13**, 152-7

Boland, L. [1977a] 'Testability in economic science' **South African Journal of Economics, 45**, 93-105

Boland, L. [1977b] 'Time, testability, and equilibrium stability' **Atlantic Economic Journal, 5**, 39-47

Boland, L. [1977c] 'Model specifications and stochasticism in economic methodology' **South African Journal of Economics, 45**, 182-9

Boland, L. [1977d] 'Giffen goods, market prices and testability' **Australian Economic Papers, 16**, 72-85

Boland, L. [1979a] 'A critique of Friedman's critics' **Journal of Economic Literature, 17**, 503-22

Boland, L. [1979b] 'Knowledge and the role of institutions in economic theory' **Journal of Economic Issues, 8**, 957-72

Boland, L. [1980] 'Friedman's methodology vs. conventional empiricism: a reply to Rotwein' **Journal of Economic Literature, 18**, 1555-7

Boland, L. [1981a] 'Satisficing in methodology: a reply to Rendigs Fels' **Journal of Economic Literature, 19**, 84-6

Boland, L. [1981b] 'On the futility of criticizing the neoclassical maximization hypothesis' **American Economic Review, 71**, 1031-6

Boland, L. [1982] **Foundations of Economic Method** (London: Geo. Allen & Unwin)

Boland, L. [1983] 'Reply to Caldwell' **American Economic Review, 73,** 828-30

Boland, L. [1984] 'Methodology: reply' **American Economic Review, 74,** 795-7

Boland, L. [1986] **Methodology for a New Microeconomics** (Boston: Allen & Unwin)

Brems, H. [1959] **Output, Employment, Capital and Growth: A Quantitative Analysis** (New York: Harper)

Briefs, H. [1960] **Three Views of Method in Economics** (Washington: Georgetown University Press)

Brodbeck, M. (ed.) [1968] **Readings in the Philosophy of the Social Sciences** (London: Collier-Macmillan)

Bronfenbrenner, M. [1966] 'A "middlebrow" introduction to economic methodology' in Krupp [1966], 4-24

Brown, K. (ed.) [1965] **Hobbes' Studies** (Oxford: Basil Blackwell)

Bunge, M. (ed.) [1964] **The Critical Approach in Science and Philosophy** (London: Collier-Macmillan)

Caldwell, B. [1982] **Beyond Positivism** (London: Geo. Allen & Unwin)

Chamberlin, E. [1933] **The Theory of Monopolistic Competition** (Cambridge: Harvard University Press)

Charlesworth, J. (ed.) [1963] **Mathematics and the Social Sciences** (Philadelphia: American Academy of Political and Social Sciences)

Clower, R. [1959] 'Some theory of an ignorant monopolist' **Economic Journal, 69,** 705-16

Clower, R. and J. Due [1972] **Microeconomics** (Homewood: Irwin)

De Alessi, L. [1965] 'Economic theory as a language' **Quarterly Journal of Economics, 19,** 472-7

De Alessi, L. [1971] 'Reversals of assumptions and implications' **Journal of Political Economy, 79,** 867-77

Debreu, G. [1959] **Theory of Value: An Axiomatic Analysis of Economic Equilibrium** (New York: Wiley)

Dorfman, R., P. Samuelson and R. Solow [1958] **Linear Programming and Economic Analysis** (New York: McGraw-Hill)

Duhem, P. [1906/62] **The Aim and Structure of Physical Theory** (New York: Atheneum)

Eddington, A. [1958] **Philosophy of Physical Science** (Ann Arbor: University of Michigan Press)

Einstein, A. [1950] **Out of My Later Years** (New York: The Wisdom Library)

Einstein, A. and L. Infeld [1938/61] **The Evolution of Physics: The Growth of Ideas from Early Concepts to Relativity and Quanta** (New York: Simon & Schuster)

Ellis, H. (ed.) [1948] **A Survey of Contemporary Economics** (Homewood: Irwin)

Enthoven, A. [1963] 'Economic analysis of the Department of Defense' **American Economic Review, Papers and Proceedings, 53,** 413-23

Ferguson, C. [1972] **Microeconomic Theory**, 3rd edn (Homewood: Irwin)

Finger, J. [1971] 'Is equilibrium an operational concept?' **Economic Journal, 81**, 609-12

Fisher, F. [1966] **The Identification Problem in Econometrics** (New York: McGraw-Hill)

Friedman, M. [1953] 'The methodology of positive economics' in **Essays in Positive Economics** (Chicago: University of Chicago Press), 3-43

Gale, D. [1955] 'The law of supply and demand' **Mathematica Scandinavica, 3**, 155-69

Georgescu-Roegen, N. [1954] 'Choice and revealed preference' **Southern Economic Journal, 21**, 119-30

Georgescu-Roegen, N. [1966] **Analytical Economics: Issues and Problems** (Cambridge: Harvard University Press)

Georgescu-Roegen, N. [1971] **The Entropy Law and the Economic Process** (Cambridge: Harvard University Press)

Goldberger, A. [1964] **Econometric Theory** (New York: Wiley)

Gordon, D. [1955a] 'Operational propositions in economic theory' **Journal of Political Economy, 63**, 150-62

Gordon, D. [1955b] 'Professor Samuelson on operationalism in economic theory' **Quarterly Journal of Economics, 63**, 305-10

Grubel, H. and L. Boland [1986] 'On the efficient use of mathematics in economics: some theory, facts and results of an opinion survey' **Kyklos, 39**, 419-42

Haavelmo, T. [1941/44] 'Probability approach to econometrics' **Econometrica, 12**, Supplement

Haavelmo, T. [1943] 'The statistical implication of a system of simultaneous equations' **Econometrica, 11**, 1-12

Hahn, F. [1965a] 'Introduction' in Hahn and Brechling [1965], xi-xv

Hahn, F. [1965b] 'On some problems of proving the existence of an equilibrium in a monetary economy' in Hahn and Brechling [1965], 126-35

Hahn, F. [1973] **On the Notion of Equilibrium in Economics** (Cambridge: Cambridge University Press)

Hahn, F. and F.P.R. Brechling (eds) [1965] **The Theory of Interest Rates: Proceedings of a Conference Held by the International Economics Association** (London: Macmillan)

Hansen, B. [1970] **A Survey of General Equilibrium Systems** (New York: McGraw-Hill)

Hendry, D. [1983] 'Comment' (on MacKinnon [1983]) **Econometric Reviews, 2**, 111-14

Hicks, J. [1939/46] **Value and Capital** (Oxford: Clarendon Press)

Hicks, J. [1956] **A Revision of Demand Theory** (Oxford: Clarendon Press)

Hicks, J. [1979] **Causality in Economics** (Oxford: Basil Blackwell)

Hood, W. and T. Koopmans (eds) [1953] **Studies in Econometric Method** (New York: Wiley)

Hurewicz, W. and H. Wallman [1948] **Dimension Theory** (Princeton: Princeton University Press)

Hutchison, T. [1938] **The Significance and Basic Postulates of Economic Theory** (London: Macmillan)

Hutchison, T. [1956] 'Professor Machlup on verification in economics' **Southern Economic Journal, 22**, 476-83

Hutchison, T. [1960] 'Methodological prescriptions in economics: a reply' **Economica, 27 (NS)**, 158-61

Jensen, K., S. Kamath and R. Bennett [1987] 'Money in the production function: an alternative test procedure' **Eastern Economic Journal, 13**, 259-69

Johnston, J. [1963] **Econometric Methods** (New York: McGraw-Hill)

Kaldor, N. [1972] 'The irrelevance of equilibrium economics' **Economic Journal, 82**, 1237-55

Kennedy, P. [1979/85] **A Guide to Econometrics**, 2nd edn (Oxford: Basil Blackwell)

Keynes, J.M. [1936] **General Theory of Employment, Interest and Money** (New York: Harcourt, Brace & World)

Klappholz, K. and J. Agassi [1959] 'Methodological prescriptions in economics' **Economica, 26 (NS)**, 60-74

Klein, L. [1957] 'The scope and limitations of econometrics' **Applied Statistics, 6**, 1-17

Koopmans, T. [1941] 'The logic of econometric business cycle research' **Journal of Political Economy, 49**, 157-81

Koopmans, T. (ed.) [1950a] **Statistical Inference in Dynamic Economic Models** (New York: Wiley)

Koopmans, T. [1950b] 'When is an equation system complete for statistical purposes?' in Koopmans [1950a], 393-409

Koopmans, T. [1953] 'Identification problems in economic model construction' in Hood and Koopmans [1953], 27-48

Koopmans, T. [1957] **Three Essays on the State of Economic Science** (New York: McGraw-Hill)

Koopmans T. and W. Hood [1953] 'The estimation of simultaneous linear economic relationships' in Hood and Koopmans [1953], 112-99

Krupp, S. [1966] **The Structure of Economic Science: Essays on Methodology** (Englewood Cliffs: Prentice-Hall)

Kuenne, R. [1963] **The Theory of General Economic Equilibrium** (Princeton: Princeton University Press)

Kuenne, R. (ed.) [1967] **Monopolistic Competition Theory: Studies in Impact** (New York: Wiley)

Kuhn, H. [1956] 'On a theorem of Wald' in Kuhn and Tucker [1965], 265-74

Kuhn, H. and A.W. Tucker (eds) [1956] **Linear Inequalities and Related Systems** (Princeton: Princeton University Press)

Kuhn, T. [1962/70] **The Structure of Scientific Revolutions** (Chicago: University of Chicago Press)

Lakatos, I. and A. Musgrave (eds) [1968] **Problems in the Philosophy of Science** (Amsterdam: North Holland)

Lancaster, K. [1966] 'A new approach to consumer theory' **Journal of Political Economy, 74**, 132-57

Leontief, W. [1948] 'Econometrics' in Ellis [1948], 388-411

Lerner, A. [1944] **The Economics of Control: Principles of Welfare Economics** (London: Macmillan)

Liebhafsky, H. [1963] **The Nature of Price Theory** (Homewood: Dorsey Press)

Lipsey, R. [1963] **An Introduction to Positive Economics** (London: Weidenfeld & Nicolson)

Lipsey, R. and K. Lancaster [1956-7] 'The general theory of second best' **Review of Economic Studies, 24**, 11-32

Lipsey, R. and P. Steiner [1972] **Economics** (New York: Harper & Row)

Lloyd, C. [1965] 'On the falsifiability of traditional demand theory' **Metroeconomica, 17**, 17-23

Lloyd, C. [1967] **Microeconomic Analysis** (Homewood: Irwin)

Lloyd, C. [1969] 'Ceteris paribus, etc.' **Metroeconomica, 21**, 86-9

Loasby, B. [1981] 'Hypothesis and paradigm in the theory of the firm' **Economic Journal, 81**, 863-85

Machlup, F. [1955] 'The problem of verification in economics' **Southern Economic Journal, 22**, 1-21

Machlup, F. [1966] 'Operationalism and pure theory in economics' in Krupp [1966], 53-67

MacKinnon, J. [1983] 'Model specification tests against non-nested alternatives' **Econometric Reviews, 2**, 85-110

Mann, H. and A. Wald [1943] 'On the statistical treatment of linear stochastic difference equations' **Econometrica, 11**, 173-220

de Marchi, N. [1985/88] 'Popper and the LSE economists' in de Marchi [1988], 139-66

de Marchi, N. (ed.) [1988] **The Popperian Legacy in Economics** (Cambridge: Cambridge University Press)

Marschak, J. [1953] 'Economic measurements for policy and prediction' in Hood and Koopmans [1953], 1-26

Marshall, A. [1890/1920] **Principles of Economics**, 8th edn (London: Macmillan)

Massey, G. [1965] 'Professor Samuelson on theory and realism: comment' **American Economic Review, 55**, 1155-64

McCloskey, D. [1983] 'The rhetoric of economics' **Journal of Economic Literature, 21**, 481-517

McKenzie, L. [1954] 'On equilibrium in Graham's model of world trade and other competitive systems' **Econometrica, 22**, 147-61

McManus, M. [1959] 'Comments on the general theory of the second best' **Review of Economic Studies, 24**, 209-24

Meade, J. [1955] **Trade and Welfare** (Oxford: Oxford University Press)

Metzler, L. [1948] review of Samuelson [1947/65], **American Economic Review, 38**, 905-10

Mishan, E. [1960] 'Survey of welfare economics' **Economic Journal, 70**, 197-265

Mishan, E. [1964] **Welfare Economics** (New York: Random House)

Morgenstern, O. [1963] 'Limits to the uses of mathematics in economics' in Charlesworth [1963], 12-29

Morgenstern, O. [1972] 'Thirteen critical points in contemporary economic theory: an interpretation' **Journal of Economic Literature, 10**, 1163-89

Nagel, E. [1961] **Structure of Science: Problems in the Logic of Scientific Explanation** (New York: Harcourt Brace)

Nikaido, H. [1956] 'On the classical multilateral exchange problem' **Metroeconomica, 8,** 135-45

Nikaido, H. [1960/70] **Introduction to Sets and Mappings in Modern Economics** (Amsterdam: North Holland)

Papandreou, A. [1958] **Economics as a Science** (New York: Lippincott Company)

Papandreou, A. [1963] 'Theory construction and empirical meaning in economics' **American Economic Review, Papers and Proceedings, 53,** 205-10

Pesaran, M. [1974] 'On the general problem of model selection' **Review of Economic Studies, 41,** 153-71

Pigou, A. [1962] **The Economics of Welfare** (London: Macmillan)

Poincaré, H. [1905/52] **Science and Hypothesis** (New York: Dover)

Popper, K. [1945/62] **The Open Society and Its Enemies** (London: Routledge & Kegan Paul)

Popper, K. [1959/61] **The Logic of Scientific Discovery** (New York: Science Editions, Inc.)

Popper, K. [1965] **Conjectures and Refutations: The Growth of Scientific Knowledge** (New York: Basic Books)

Popper, K. [1972] **Objective Knowledge** (London: Oxford University Press)

Quine, W. [1965] **Elementary Logic** rev. edn (New York: Harper & Row)

Quine, W. [1972] **Methods of Logic** (New York: Holt, Rinehart & Winston)

Richardson, G. [1959] 'Equilibrium, expectations and information' **Economic Journal, 69,** 225-37

Robinson, J. [1933] **Economics of Imperfect Competition** (London: Macmillan)

Robinson, J. [1962] **Economic Philosophy** (London: Watts)

Rotwein, E. [1959] 'On "The methodology of positive economics"' **Quarterly Journal of Economics, 73,** 554-75

Rotwein, E. [1966] 'Mathematical economics: the empirical view and an appeal for pluralism' in Krupp [1966], 102-13

Salmon, G. [1928] **A Treatise on the Analytic Geometry of Three Dimensions** (London: Longmans, Green & Company)

Samuelson, P. [1938] 'The empirical implications of utility analysis' **Econometrica, 6,** 344-56

Samuelson, P. [1947/65] **Foundations of Economic Analysis** (New York: Atheneum)

Samuelson, P. [1947-8] 'Some implications of "linearity"' **Review of Economic Studies, 15,** 88-90

Samuelson, P. [1948] 'Consumption theory in terms of revealed preference' **Economica, 15** (NS), 243-53

Samuelson, P. [1950a] 'The problem of integrability in utility theory' **Economica, 17** (NS), 355-85

Samuelson, P. [1950b] 'Evaluation of real national income' **Oxford Economic Papers, 2** (NS), 1-29

Samuelson, P. [1952] 'Economic theory and mathematics – an appraisal' **American Economic Review, 42,** 56-66

Samuelson, P. [1953] 'Consumption theorems in terms of over-compensation rather than indifference comparisons' **Economica, 20 (NS),** 1-9

Samuelson, P. [1955] 'Professor Samuelson on operationalism in economic theory: comment' **Quarterly Journal of Economics, 63,** 310-14

Samuelson, P. [1962/66] 'Problems of the American economy: an economist's view' Stamp Memorial Lecture (London: The Athlone Press) reprinted in Stiglitz [1966], 1656-81

Samuelson, P. [1963] 'Problems of methodology: discussion' **American Economic Review, Papers and Proceedings, 53,** 231-6

Samuelson, P. [1963/66] 'Modern economic realities and individualism' in Stiglitz [1966], 1407-18

Samuelson, P. [1964] 'Theory and realism: a reply' **American Economic Review, 54,** 736-9

Samuelson, P. [1965] 'Professor Samuelson on theory and realism: reply' **American Economic Review, 55,** 1164-72

Samuelson, P. [1967] 'Monopolistic competition revolution' in Kuenne [1967], 105-38

Samuelson, P. [1983] **Foundations of Economic Analysis,** 3rd edn (Cambridge: Harvard University Press)

Samuelson, P. and A. Scott [1971] **Economics,** 3rd Canadian edn, (Toronto: McGraw-Hill)

Sassower, R. [1985] **Philosophy of Economics: A Critique of Demarcation** (New York: University Press of America)

Shapiro, H. [1973] 'Is verification possible? The evaluation of large econometric models' **American Journal of Agricultural Economics, 55,** 250-8

Simon, H. [1953] 'Causal ordering and identifiability' in Hood and Koopmans [1953], 49-74

Simon, H. [1963] 'Problems of methodology: discussion' **American Economic Review, Papers and Proceedings, 53,** 229-31

Smith, V.K. [1969] 'The identification problem and the validity of economic models: a comment' **South African Journal of Economics, 37,** 81

Stigler, G. [1949] **Five Lectures on Economic Problems** (London: Macmillan)

Stigler, G. [1963] 'Archibald vs. Chicago' **Review of Economic Studies, 30,** 63-4

Stiglitz, J. (ed.) [1966] **Collected Papers of Paul A. Samuelson** (Cambridge: MIT Press)

Swamy, P.A.V.B., R. Conway and P. von zur Muehlen [1985] 'The foundations of econometrics – are there any?' **Econometric Reviews, 4,** 1-61

Tarascio, V. and B. Caldwell [1979] 'Theory choice in economics: philosophy and practice' **Journal of Economic Issues, 13,** 983-1006

Tinbergen, J. [1956/67] **Economic Policy: Principles and Design** (Amsterdam: North Holland)

Wald, A. [1936/51] 'On some systems of equations of mathematical economics' **Econometrica, 19,** 368-403

Ward, B. [1972] **What's Wrong with Economics?** (New York: Basic Books)

Wartofsky, M. [1968] **Conceptual Foundations of Scientific Thought** (New York: Collier-Macmillan)

Watkins, J. [1957] 'Between analytic and empirical' **Philosophy, 32**, 112-31

Watkins, J. [1965] 'Philosophy and politics in Hobbes' in Brown [1965], 237-62

Wedeking, G. [1969] 'Duhem, Quine and Grunbaum on falsification' **Philosophy of Science, 36**, 375-80

Weintraub, E.R. [1985] **General Equilibrium Analysis** (Cambridge: Cambridge University Press)

Wilson, C. [1963] **The Outsider** (London: Pan Books)

Wong, S. [1973] 'The "F-twist" and the methodology of Paul Samuelson' **American Economic Review, 63**, 312-25

Wong, S. [1978] **The Foundations of Paul Samuelson's Revealed Preference Theory** (London: Routledge & Kegan Paul)

Woods, F. [1961] **Higher Geometry: An Introduction to Advanced Methods in Analytic Geometry** (New York: Dover)

Zeuthen, F. [1957] **Economic Theory and Method** (Cambridge: Harvard University Press)

Names Index

Subject Index